T0356878

A WORKBOOK TO HELP YOU BALANCE EMOTIONS
& TAKE CHARGE OF YOUR MENTAL HEALTH

THOUGHTS
& FEELINGS
FOR TEENS

ELISA NEBOLSINE, LCSW

Instant Help Books
An Imprint of New Harbinger Publications, Inc.

Publisher's Note

INSTANT HELP, the Clock Logo, and NEW HARBINGER are trademarks of New Harbinger Publications, Inc.

New Harbinger Publications is an employee-owned company.

Copyright © 2025 by Elisa Nebolsine
Instant Help Books
An imprint of New Harbinger Publications, Inc.
5720 Shattuck Avenue
Oakland, CA 94609
www.newharbinger.com

All Rights Reserved

Cover design by Amy Shoup

Interior design by Tom Comitta

Acquired by Jess O'Brien

Edited by Meaghan McDermott

Library of Congress Cataloging-in-Publication Data on file

FSC
www.fsc.org
MIX
Paper | Supporting
responsible forestry
FSC® C008955

Printed in the United States of America

27   26   25

10   9   8   7   6   5   4   3   2   1   First Printing

"Elisa Nebolsine's *Thoughts and Feelings for Teens* is an excellent manual that demonstrates the principles of cognitive behavioral therapy (CBT), and provides valuable materials for adolescents. This workbook effectively teaches adolescents how to implement evidence-based strategies to deal with difficult emotions, manage anxiety, and build resilience and emotional strength. Elisa has done a great job of explaining the concepts in a straightforward, nonthreatening manner, allowing readers to recognize their thoughts and feelings and learn how to deal with them effectively. This book should be read by every teen, their parents, and the people who work with them."

—*Judith Beck*, clinical professor of psychology at the University of Pennsylvania; and president of the Beck Institute for Cognitive Behavior Therapy, a nonprofit that does virtual national and international training

"Elisa Nebolsine writes with the expertise of a seasoned therapist, yet comes across like a trusted, older friend who truly 'gets' the teen experience. Adolescents struggling with challenging thoughts, intense emotions, and everyday stressors will find the guidance and tools in this workbook both accessible and empowering. I highly recommend it!"

—*Marci Fox, PhD*, licensed psychologist, and coauthor of *The Comprehensive Clinician's Guide to Cognitive Behavioral Therapy*

"This workbook offers teens numerous evidence-based strategies and exercises that empower them to improve their mood and well-being by managing thoughts and emotions, and finding the courage to take action. I found the exercises inspiring teens to create their own timeline of awesomeness and to 'unlock' their self-compassion particularly compelling."

—*Mary Alvord, PhD*, psychologist; founder of Alvord, Baker & Associates and Resilience Across Borders; and coauthor of *The Action Mindset Workbook for Teens*, *Conquer Negative Thinking for Teens*, and *Resilience Builder Program*

"Elisa Nebolsine's *Thoughts and Feelings for Teens* is a game changer for young people navigating life's emotional challenges. Packed with proven CBT tools, this engaging and compassionate workbook empowers teens to build resilience, manage emotions, and thrive. It is a necessary tool for anyone supporting the mental health of today's youth."

—*Beth Salcedo, MD*, past president of the Anxiety and Depression Association of America (ADAA), medical director of The Ross Center, and distinguished fellow of the American Psychological Association (APA)

"Elisa Nebolsine's *Thoughts and Feelings for Teens* is an outstanding resource that empowers young readers to take charge of their mental health with clarity and compassion. Drawing from evidence-based practices, this workbook introduces teens to practical tools for managing emotions, reducing anxiety, and building resilience. Elisa's approachable style makes complex concepts accessible, fostering growth and confidence in her readers. This workbook is an invaluable guide for teens, and a trusted resource for clinicians and educators supporting them."

—*Melissa D. Grady, PhD*, professor of social work at Catholic University, and author of *Moving Beyond Assessment*

"*Thoughts and Feelings for Teens* is an exceptional workbook that offers adolescents practical and evidence-based strategies to navigate the complexities of today's world. Elisa Nebolsine blends techniques from CBT, acceptance and commitment therapy (ACT), and dialectical behavior therapy (DBT) to empower teens to take charge of their mental health. It's an invaluable resource for any teen looking to build resilience and achieve their goals."

—*Amy Wenzel, PhD*, founder and director of the Main Line Center for Evidence-Based Psychotherapy

"This workbook is so wonderful! In it, teens who are struggling with big emotions will find clear and direct instructions to help them understand why they are having those big feelings, and how to navigate them. In each chapter, Elisa Nebolsine provides strategies to support a specific skill with examples, explanations, and thoughtfully constructed worksheets. I love everything about this book."

—*Sarah Wayland, PhD*, founder of Guiding Exceptional Parents, cofounder of The Behavior Revolution, and coauthor of *Is This Autism?*

CONTENTS

FOREWORD

Thoughts and Feelings: Taking Control of Your Moods and Life has provided generations of readers with powerful ways to handle the many challenges life throws us all. It offers actionable tools and an array of proven-effective psychological techniques in one place, so just about anyone can improve their life and increase their mental health.

In this book, Elisa Nebolsine, LCSW, brings these skills to teen readers who need them. Getting an early grasp on basic knowledge of how your mind and emotions work will help you build fortitude and resilience for the years to come.

This workbook offers simple, step-by-step instructions for ten of the best, most powerful techniques drawn from cognitive behavior therapy. Millions of people have used these skills to cope with the problems they face, such as unwanted thoughts, anxiety, and mental distress.

Pick out the techniques that apply to your situation or just start from the beginning and work your way through. The thoughtful descriptions, examples, and practical advice offered here will give you what you need to make a real difference in your mental health.

Thoughts and Feelings was written because life is hard. We all start off facing our daily struggles with what we've randomly learned from parents, family, friends, and teachers. Some of this has been helpful, some not. This book is about tools that work, that help you change old patterns, to take control of your moods and your life.

—Matthew McKay, PhD

INTRODUCTION

Charting Your Course: Creating a Plan for Change

"It's not what happens to you, but how you react to it that matters."

—Epictetus

If you're reading this book, chances are you're struggling. Whether you're facing sadness, anxiety, or waves of big emotions, know this: you're not alone. It is so hard to feel so bad.

This book is here to offer a path toward feeling better. But just as important, it's completely valid to feel whatever you are experiencing at this moment—whatever you are feeling is okay. While I may not know exactly what you're going through, I genuinely care, and I'm supporting you on this journey from afar.

The information in this book is based on research, and it reflects strategies that professionals in this field know can help. I wish you could just take a class at school to learn the latest ways to improve your mood, lower stress, and handle emotions, but since most schools don't offer one, this book aims to fill that gap. This workbook is not a replacement for expert help, but it will give you tools to take control of how you feel. Think of this as a DIY guide for learning to feel and live better.

As you turn these pages, you'll find activities, worksheets, and thought exercises—think of them as your personal toolkit for tough times. Each chapter builds on the last, giving you a step-by-step approach to navigate through heavy feelings, but you don't have to do them all in order. You also might find some strategies work better for you than others, and that's completely okay. It's all about discovering what works for you, at your own pace, in your own space. This is your journey to feeling more in charge of your emotional world, and every step forward is progress.

WELCOME TO YOUR PERSONAL GUIDE TO FEELING BETTER!

This book is like a DIY kit for your mind. It's packed with tools that you can use to make positive changes that will help you feel better. Not everything in this workbook will click, but you'll likely find parts that feel like they're talking about you. You don't need to read the workbook cover to cover, but it might be useful to check out each chapter. The first two chapters are key because they lay the groundwork and give you a base to get the most out of the rest of the workbook.

In the section below, please take a minute to write down your goals for this book. What do you most hope to get out of it? I know it's annoying to keep talking about research, but there are studies that show that when we write down our goals with intention, we actually are more likely to create the changes.

WHAT ARE YOUR GOALS?

What are the main feelings or challenges you want to work on? Think about what's been on your mind lately, what feelings have been challenging, and what situations you wish you could redo.

_____

_____

_____

How do these challenges affect your daily life? Consider how your feelings or situations impact your schoolwork, friendships, family, and extracurricular activities. Understanding this can help you see what changes might make a big difference for you.

_____

_____

_____

What does a good day look like to you? Imagine a day where you wake up feeling better (maybe even excellent). What's different on this day? **Describe what you're doing, how you're feeling, and who you're with.**

What skills are you most interested in learning from this workbook to help you feel better? This might include learning how to manage stress, improving your thoughts about yourself, or finding ways to deal with difficult emotions.

How will you know if you're making progress? Think about signs that things are getting better for you. This might include feeling happier, getting more done, or handling tough situations more easily. It's also okay if these signs change over time.

In this workbook, you are going to learn solid, research-backed ways to shift your thoughts, feelings, and actions. I wish I could say that you will immediately feel better, but unfortunately this isn't magic and the changes won't happen instantly. If you practice, the changes will happen. The more you work on these techniques, the better you'll feel. It's like leveling up in a game—the more you play, the stronger you get.

So, while our brains don't come with an instant fix button, you can learn these skills and have them ready for whatever life throws at you. And, if you're reading this book, my guess is that you've experienced how hard things can get. I'm sorry that's happened, and I wish it hadn't. Life is rough, and the more we know about our emotions, thoughts, and our brains, the more we can do to feel better. Once you learn these skills, they become super-useful and they are always available to help. You will likely notice that you begin to feel a little different and hopefully a lot better.

Starting something new can be tough. It might help to team up with a friend, relative, or trusted person to try out the exercises or just to keep you on track. If you want some extra guidance, talking to a therapist trained in these techniques can help. They can help you tailor a treatment plan, provide accountability, and support you along the way. And, remember that this book isn't a substitute for professional help. If you need more support, please reach out to a trusted adult—a parent, guardian, school counselor, teacher, or another adult to help you get connected to a therapist. You don't have to do this alone, and there are good people out there who can help. The best way to start is by asking for help.

UNDERSTANDING YOUR TOOLKIT: CBT, ACT, AND DBT EXPLAINED

There are lots of different kinds of therapy and ways to help people with their thoughts and feelings. This book mainly uses tools from three of them: cognitive behavioral therapy (CBT), acceptance and commitment therapy (ACT), and dialectical behavior therapy (DBT). Let's take a look at each one to understand how they work.

What Is Cognitive Behavioral Therapy (CBT)?

When you think of therapy, you might imagine the old-school image of lying on a couch while a therapist sits behind you taking notes. CBT isn't like that. It's active and focused on the here and now. The core idea of CBT is that your thoughts about a situation shape how you see the event. The event itself often matters less than the way you think about the event.

In other words, it's not what happens to you that counts, but how think about it, how you react to it, and how you perceive it. You can't control everything that happens to you, but you can control how you respond. Changing your perspective on a situation can change everything.

CBT teaches you to see things in a way that's both true and helpful. This doesn't mean faking happiness or lying to yourself. It's about shifting your thoughts from something like, "This is the worst. I can't handle it," to a true and helpful view like, "This is tough, but I've gotten through tough times before. I know I can do hard things." When our thoughts focus on our strengths instead of our fears, it changes how we feel and what we do. We also gain understanding about our deeper beliefs through our thoughts, and through catching, checking, and changing our thoughts, we learn more about ourselves.

What Is Acceptance and Commitment Therapy (ACT)?

ACT (it's pronounced like the word "act") teaches you how to live a richer, more meaningful life, even when you are facing difficult situations and emotions. In ACT, the focus is on accepting things that are out of your control. You don't give up and just say that everything going wrong is fine, but you do acknowledge the difficulties without letting them control you and your life. For example, if you're feeling really anxious about a test, ACT doesn't try to get rid of your anxiety. Instead, it helps you accept that you're anxious but still able to focus on studying. I know, it sounds weird, but you might say, "I am anxious, it's okay that I'm anxious, but I still choose to study," rather than the default "I am way too anxious to study right now; I'll just watch a little Netflix and then see how I feel."

Being present in the moment is super-important in ACT. In ACT, you stay focused on the present and avoid getting stuck in the past or stressing too much about the future. For example, if you're hanging out with friends, you may find your thoughts going to a test next week, homework you still need to turn in, or a big fight with your mom that morning. We all do this, but ACT teaches us to pull our thoughts back to the present moment. You learn to let your mind to drop into what is going on right now in this moment. ACT teaches you to enjoy the friend experience and not miss out on the moment because your mind is somewhere else. ACT skills teach you to stay in the now to fully experience life as it happens.

Another key part of ACT is figuring out what really matters to you—your values. Values are like your personal compass; they guide you in deciding how you want to live your life. Maybe kindness, courage, or being a good friend are essential values for you. Whatever your values, ACT helps you take actions that match these values, even when it's hard. Once you understand your values, you focus on "committed action." This means taking steps toward living according to your values, even when life gets tough.

ACT isn't about getting rid of bad feelings or changing difficult situations directly. It's about learning to live a fulfilling life, with all its ups and downs, guided by what's truly important to you.

What Is Dialectical Behavior Therapy (DBT)?

DBT is a type of therapy designed to help you manage emotions and improve relationships. Two ideas are central to DBT: balance and change. When you have balance, you are able to accept your feelings, but also able to recognize that you may need to act differently when you have these feelings. Balance, in DBT, is about being able to identify the emotion or emotions that you are experiencing in the moment. It also means that you understand that how you express your emotions affects both you and the people around you.

Change is the other key concept in DBT. In DBT, change means recognizing what's not going well for you and learning to respond to it in a better way. It's important not to confuse change with changing who you are. You are wonderful. Change is about transforming the ways you handle emotions and experiences that don't help you, but never about changing what makes you uniquely you. DBT provides a set of tools that help you gradually and effectively learn to make these changes.

In DBT, balance and change are achieved through practical skills. The model emphasizes specific strategies like mindfulness to be more aware in the moment, distress tolerance to help you deal with discomfort without making it worse, and emotion regulation to help you understand and manage your feelings. As you learn and practice these skills, you create a balance between acceptance (life right now) and change (taking steps to make life the way you want it to be).

In DBT, the blend of balance and change lets you navigate life's ups and downs with a sense of control and direction. By practicing mindfulness, you learn to observe your experiences without getting lost in them, creating space to choose your responses. Through distress tolerance, you'll discover how to face uncomfortable situations without making them harder than they need to be. When you learn to manage your emotions, you start to understand your feelings better. This understanding helps you change your response to big or overwhelming feelings, which in turn gives you greater control over your emotions. All of this means that you're not ruled by quick reactions, but can slow down and make decisions that help you move forward with confidence and purpose.

ONWARD!

You now have an overview of this workbook and a basic idea of the theories of CBT, ACT, and DBT. CBT will teach you that it's not just what happens to you, but your thoughts about it that shape your world. ACT will help you learn the power of accepting your feelings and committing to actions that align with your values. And DBT will provide a balanced and skill-based approach, helping you navigate emotions and relationships with a steadier hand.

As you turn the page and move into the rest of the workbook, you're beginning to chart your own course. This means taking these therapies' principles and crafting a personal plan that resonates with your life, your challenges, and your dreams. I hope you can craft a sense of meaning in your actions and build a life that not only feels better but is also truer to who you are. (I have to reiterate, you are wonderful.)

Each chapter ahead is a step on this course. You'll find activities and insights that help you move to a more mindful, resilient, and meaningful life. The worksheets are also available online at **http://newharbinger.com/54513**. Feel free to print out multiple copies and do an exercise more than once. As you explore, remember: you're in the driver's seat, and you get to choose the route that works best for you.

Let's get started. Use the strategies from CBT to reshape unhelpful thoughts. Let ACT remind you to embrace your experiences and act according to your deepest values. Allow DBT to teach you the balance of acceptance and change. With each skill you master, you'll be defining and refining your course, discovering that the greatest adventure is the journey within (really!).

Ready? Let's begin.

CHAPTER 1
AUTOMATIC THOUGHTS

Uncovering the Messages in Your Mind

Sam is a fifteen-year-old who loves skateboarding and hanging out with friends, but despite his laidback appearance he worries a lot about being included and fitting in. Sam texts his best friend to see if he can hang out this weekend, and the friend responds just with "No, sorry." Sam immediately thinks, "He doesn't want to spend time with me; he's probably hanging out with other people without me." Sam is convinced the friend just doesn't want to see him, and his negative automatic thoughts (NATs) lead him to feel angry and hurt by his belief that his friend is blowing him off.

In reality, the friend who sent the text is dealing with a serious family situation, and the reason they can't hang out has nothing to do with Sam. Because Sam believed the NAT without checking it or trying to change it, he was unintentionally unsupportive of his friend and got himself into a negative spiral that was based on false assumptions. If Sam had been able to catch and check his NATs, as you will learn below, he could have handled the situation in a very different way.

We are all constantly thinking. Even when we try not to think, we end up thinking. Some estimates say that people have as many as 10,000 thoughts in one day. And your thoughts are important. Thoughts narrate experiences; how you think about an event shapes how you feel about and understand that experience. In other words, the real issue isn't what actually happened; rather, what matters most is how you understand and interpret that experience.

In cognitive behavioral therapy, thoughts, specifically *negative automatic thoughts* (NATs), are super-important. NATs are the immediate thoughts that pop up in our minds in response to a situation. These thoughts tend to be more skewed to the negative, and they influence how we feel and act.

HOW IT WORKS

NATs can be powerful and misleading. If you just let them keep going, it's like having a song on repeat in your mind. Before long, you know all of the words by heart and can recite them without even trying. You don't want or benefit from your most negative thoughts repeating over and over in your mind. When those NATS take over it often leads to heavy and uncomfortable emotions that make the thoughts feel true even when they aren't.

The first step to changing NATS is to notice that they are happening. This simple step makes a big difference. Instead of just reacting to the NATS and ending up feeling hurt, saying the wrong thing, or acting awkward, you can learn to check the thoughts and even change them before you overreact.

Let's take a look at some common NATs. You may or may not recognize these as thoughts you have, but it gives you a sense of how NATs sound:

SELF-CRITICAL: "I'm not good enough," "I'm a failure," or "I can't do anything right."

APPROVAL SEEKING: "They think I am so weird," "They are totally judging me," or "I have to make them like me."

PERFECTIONIST: "If I don't get this just right, it isn't worth doing," "Anything less than an A is pretty much failing," or "I always mess up and ruin everything."

WORTH: "I don't deserve for things to go well," "I don't deserve to have a boy/girlfriend," or "I'm not good enough/not enough."

COMPARISON: "I will never look that good," "They have such a good life compared to me," or "I'll never be as smart as them."

HOPELESSNESS: "I'm not capable of change," "It won't ever get better," or "There's no point in trying."

UNLIKABILITY: "They won't reply if I text," "They don't want to hang out with me," or "Why bother trying? No one likes me anyway."

Here's an example: Sam is a strong student, but he did badly on a test. His response: total panic. His NATs are: "I am terrible at math," "I'll never get this," and "I'm just not smart enough."

These automatic thoughts influence how he feels and how he acts. His thoughts are negative, permanent, and pessimistic, and he may not even notice that he is thinking this way. These thoughts matter because Sam's brain believes them. If Sam tells himself that he is terrible at math, unable to learn, and not smart enough, he sends his brain and body into a state of distress. The more he thinks these thoughts, the more stress he feels, and that leads him down a rabbit hole of deeper and darker thoughts.

If Sam accepts his NATs as true, then he is accepting a view of himself that is inaccurate and highly skewed to the negative. Why would he bother studying more if he is "never" going to get it? Why get extra help from the teacher if he's "just not smart enough"? These NATs can actually change Sam's behavior and lead to him giving up.

But, if Sam can learn to catch his negative automatic thoughts, he can start to recognize negative patterns of thinking, and he can learn to replace the NATs with thoughts that are true and helpful. For example, if Sam can catch himself thinking, "I'll never get this. I'm just not smart enough," he can pause and replace that thought with, "That test was tough, but it was just a test. Next time I am going to study harder and do better." I know, it sounds too basic, but it actually works. The more you practice it, the more it changes how you see situations. You can learn how to start in the section below.

STRATEGY: CATCH YOUR NATS

NATs are always occurring. We rarely even notice them because they are so frequent, but that's the problem. Automatic thoughts are constantly narrating our experiences, and they tell the story of how we understand situations, even when we're not really paying attention (not consciously, anyway). This sounds obvious, but in order to be in charge of our own story, we have to know what we are telling ourselves. This is why we have to catch these NATs.

EXERCISE CATCH YOUR NATS

Recall a situation in the past week that was difficult. **Describe that situation below:**

_____

_____

_____

Think back to that time and try to recall the specific negative automatic thoughts that were playing in your mind. It can be tough to remember the specific thoughts, and that's okay. You don't need to have them exactly right. Just imagine the situation as it happened, play it over in your mind, and come up with the likely NATs. Remember, you need specific thoughts. For example, the thought "Everything is so annoying" is not very helpful. However, the thought "I always mess things up" is more useful because it shows a theme and pattern in your NATs. **Describe your thoughts:**

_____

_____

_____

What did you notice about your NATs? What surprised you? What didn't surprise you?

_____

_____

_____

It may have been tough to come up with the NATs, and that's okay and totally normal. Catching and changing NATs takes effort. These thoughts are always playing, and it's much easier for most of us to tune them out than it is to tune in and notice. But, when you start to make the effort to pay attention and look for them, you will start to notice them. Like any other skill, it takes practice. Once you get the hang of catching and changing NATs, it changes everything.

You're off to a great start! Catching, checking, and changing NATs is tough, and the first step—catching them—is often the hardest. Once you get the hang of this step, the rest becomes easier. Remember, NATs usually aren't really about the situation at hand; rather, they represent deeper beliefs we have about ourselves. In order to know whether the thought is true and helpful or false and harmful, we have to start to check them.

STRATEGY: CHECK YOUR NATS

The steps below are an easy way to check your thoughts. Some thoughts may be both true and false—that's okay too.

1. **IDENTIFY THE THOUGHT.** Write down the specific negative automatic thoughts (NATs) you noticed. Be as detailed as possible. *Example: Sam notices he's thinking, "Whenever I post something on social media, no one likes or comments on it. Everyone must think I'm awkward or just not even worth it."*

2. **ASK YOURSELF QUESTIONS.** Is this thought based on facts or feelings? Determine whether your thought is actually true (facts support it) or just a feeling. Remember, thoughts can be misleading and even deceiving. What are the facts? *Example: Sam asks himself whether there are facts to support his thought. He realizes it's more of a feeling because some posts do get likes and comments, just not every single one.*

3. **WHAT EVIDENCE SUPPORTS THE THOUGHT?** Look for concrete evidence that backs up your NATs. *Example: Sam recalls a time when he posted a picture and it only got a few likes. This supports his thought that some posts don't get much attention.*

4. **WHAT EVIDENCE CONTRADICTS THE THOUGHT?** Find evidence that goes against your NATs. This could be past experiences or facts that show your thought might not be entirely true. *Example: Sam remembers the post that went viral where he received so many likes and positive comments, which contradicts the thought that everyone always finds his posts boring.*

5. **CONSIDER ALTERNATIVE EXPLANATIONS.** Think of other reasons or explanations for the situation. This helps you see that your NAT might not be the only way to interpret the event. This isn't to say that your NAT can never be true, but rather to challenge the thought and explore. *Example: Sam considers that people might not always be online when he posts, or they might be busy with their own lives, and it's not necessarily about his content being boring.*

6. **DOES THIS THOUGHT HELP OR HURT YOU?** Ask yourself how this thought is affecting you. Does it make you feel anxious, sad, or unmotivated? Understanding the impact can help you see why it's important to challenge and change the thought. *Example: Sam notices that thinking everyone finds him boring makes him feel anxious and less confident about posting, which negatively impacts his mood and social interactions.*

1. **IDENTIFY THE THOUGHT.** Write down the specific negative automatic thoughts (NATs) you noticed. Be as detailed as possible.

2. **ASK YOURSELF QUESTIONS.** Is this thought based on facts or feelings? Determine whether your thought is actually true (facts support it) or just a feeling. What are the facts?

3. **WHAT EVIDENCE SUPPORTS THE THOUGHT?** Look for concrete evidence that backs up your NATs.

4. WHAT EVIDENCE CONTRADICTS THE THOUGHT? Find evidence that goes against your NATs. This could be past experiences or facts that show your thought might not be entirely true.

_____

_____

_____

_____

5. CONSIDER ALTERNATIVE EXPLANATIONS. Think of other reasons or explanations for the situation.

_____

_____

_____

_____

6. DOES THIS THOUGHT HELP OR HURT YOU? Ask yourself how this thought is affecting you.

_____

_____

_____

These steps give you the tools you need to check your NATs and see them more clearly. Your initial reaction might not be the whole truth and there are usually other, more positive and still honest ways to look at the situation.

STRATEGY: CHANGE YOUR NATS

The final step is to change the NAT. You've learned to catch them and check them against facts and evidence, and now you get to change them. This is not as easy as it sounds. The key to changing thoughts is to make sure you don't go too far to the negative or the positive; the new thoughts have to be both true and helpful.

Your brain is capable of changing thoughts. It isn't easy or quick, but you can change how your brain reacts to situations. When you begin to think in a new way, your brain makes new neural connections. The more you practice these new thoughts, the stronger these connections become. It's like building a mental muscle. Because you've been thinking a certain way for a long time, changing these patterns will take time, but adolescence is a great time to make this change. Your brain is primed for learning and quick to form new connections. By practicing the following techniques, you can create lasting change in how you think and feel. Totally worth it.

Change Your Mind Playlist

You know how a certain song can get stuck in your head, and you play it back to yourself over and over? This exercise uses that idea and switches it from song lyrics to NATs. This strategy involves learning to notice, check, and change your negative automatic thoughts. It's kind of like editing a personal playlist to include more of your favorite songs and less of the ones that bring you down.

EXERCISE | CHANGE YOUR MIND PLAYLIST, PART 1

1. Think back to some recent, tough situations, such as an offhand comment that you wish you hadn't made, when someone canceled plans on you last minute, or something awkward or embarrassing you did recently.

2. In the "Automatic Thought" section, write down the thoughts that came to mind during that event. Don't overthink; just go with what comes to mind. And, just like before, it's okay if you don't get these exactly the same as the originals.

3. In the "Feelings" section, write down every feeling that you experienced at that moment. It probably won't be five feelings, but it likely won't be just one feeling either.

4. Next, rate the feeling on a scale of 0 to 10, with 0 being no feeling and 10 being the most intense feeling you have ever experienced. Try to evaluate the emotion rating realistically, but also know that this is not an exact science.

SITUATION	AUTOMATIC THOUGHT	FEELINGS	INTENSITY RATING 0-10

EXERCISE CHANGE YOUR MIND PLAYLIST, PART 2

1. Now, look back at the situations you wrote down and consider how you could change the thought. Ask yourself:

   - Is this thought factually true, or is it just my perspective?

   - Could there be a different angle to this situation that I haven't considered?

   - What would I say to a friend who had this thought?

2. Come up with a couple of "redo" thoughts. These "redo" thoughts are true and helpful thoughts. They are more constructive and positive than the originals, but not so positive that they are unbelievable. Here are some "redo" thoughts to give you an idea.

SITUATION	NEGATIVE AUTOMATIC THOUGHT	"REDO" THOUGHT
1. I failed my math test.	I'm not smart enough.	1. If I study, I usually do well in school.
		2. I can do better if I stick with it.
2. my friend canceled our plans to see a movie.	Nobody likes me.	1. Just because one person doesn't like me, doesn't mean no one likes me.
		2. I have friends who like to spend time with me.
		3. my friend was busy and I'm just disappointed.

19

SITUATION	NEGATIVE AUTOMATIC THOUGHT	" REDO" THOUGHT
1.		1.
		2.
		3.
2.		1.
		2.
		3.

Over the next week, try to practice this every day. At the end of the week, review your entries to see if there are themes or patterns. You may be surprised at the connections you make. See what your new playlist looks like and compare it to the old one. My guess is that it's a lot more fun to listen to this new soundtrack.

Strategy: Notice Your NATs

Catching NATs can be challenging. It's so easy to forget about the thoughts and to keep on going without paying any attention to the inner narrative in our minds. One way to practice catching NATs is to literally set reminders or timers to go off throughout the day as cues to notice your NATs in that moment.

1. Set a timer or use a reminder app. At the beginning of the day, set five to seven random timers on your phone to go off throughout the day. Make sure these timers are spread out and unpredictable. For example, you might set one for mid-morning, one around lunchtime, a couple in the afternoon, and a few in the evening.

2. Create a reminder message. Set the message for each timer to something that will make you remember to catch your NATs but won't be obvious to others who might see the reminder pop up on your phone. When the timer goes off, this will be your cue to stop and check in with your thoughts.

3. Catch your NATs. When the timer goes off, pause whatever you are doing (if possible; obviously don't pause if driving!). Take a moment to notice your current thoughts and feelings. Don't rush this step. Give yourself a minute to really tune in to your thoughts. Ask yourself:

   - What was I just thinking?

   - Was it a negative thought about myself or the situation?

   - How did this thought make me feel?

4. Write it down. In your journal or notes app, jot down the negative thought you identified. Be as specific as possible. For example, instead of writing, "I feel bad," write, "I feel bad because I can't get the hang of shooting from this far away."

5. Challenge your NATs. When you have time, ideally as close to the time you caught the NAT as possible, go back and read through the NATs. For each negative thought you catch, write down a "redo" thought. Some questions that might help if you get stuck are:

- Is there another way to view this situation?

- What would I say to a friend who had this thought?

- Is this thought based on facts or feelings?

Don't worry if it feels awkward at first—it feels that way for everyone. It gets easier and easier with practice.

6. Reflect. At the end of the day, review your list of caught NATs and redo thoughts. Reflect on how this practice made you feel and whether it helped you become more aware of your thinking patterns. Write down any insights or patterns you notice. For example, do certain situations trigger more negative thoughts?

Tips

- Be honest with yourself when identifying NATs. Everyone has them, and catching them is the first step to changing them.

- Don't be discouraged if you can't think of a redo thought right away. The important part is to start noticing the patterns.

- Make this activity a daily habit to improve your self-awareness and mental well-being over time.

- Personalize your reminders to make them fun and motivating. The reminder can be something that only you know what it means.

By regularly practicing this activity, you'll become more skilled at identifying and challenging your negative thoughts, leading to a more positive and balanced outlook on life.

REFLECTIONS
REFLECTIONS

- **Your thoughts are not your destiny.** You have the power to change negative automatic thoughts that can lead to unhelpful behaviors and feelings. These thoughts can be sneaky and convincing, but by catching, checking, and changing them you get to be in charge.

- **Awareness is key.** By becoming more aware of the automatic thoughts that flit through your mind, you can start to change how you respond both through your thoughts and through your actions. This is important because it means that you can create the change you want. This might mean working harder and smarter at a task or skill, or it might mean you need to reevaluate and check to see whether the situation is truly (factually) as bad as it feels.

- **Practice, practice, practice.** Like any skill, catching and changing thoughts gets easier with practice. It's a fundamental skill in CBT that supports all of the other techniques.

- **Gain a deeper understanding.** Automatic thoughts seem basic, but they provide clues to our deeper beliefs. The better we get at recognizing and changing our automatic thoughts, the deeper our insight into what motivates our actions and feelings, and the more we learn about ourselves. This is the first step to big change!

CHAPTER 2

DON'T GET PLAYED BY YOUR BRAIN

Outsmart Your Thinking Traps

Olivia, a sophomore, sends a text to Emma, asking if she wants to get coffee after school. Emma says she would love to but can't today because she's got plans. Olivia's brain jumps to, "She's probably just dodging me. She thinks I'm weird." Her thoughts snowball from there, and in no time Olivia is convinced that Emma hates her, is avoiding her, and is telling everyone that she is weird.

Sound like something you've experienced? Have you ever jumped to the worst possible conclusion and treated it like fact? My guess is that you have. I certainly have, and I think most people know that experience. In our rational moments, we know that assuming the worst usually makes things feel much worse than they actually are, but it is so hard not to assume the worst.

Olivia was already anxious about asking Emma to hang out. When Emma wasn't immediately available, Olivia's mind spiraled. In reality, Emma was genuinely busy and asked Olivia to get coffee the next day. But in the time between Olivia's invite and Emma's counteroffer, Olivia's thoughts took off in a tornado of NATS and worries.

This is a universal human experience. Really. None of us is immune—not me, not you, not anyone. Our thoughts veer off into weird tangents that are completely inaccurate but feel absolutely true. It happens so much there's even a term for it: *cognitive distortions*. This chapter is your guide to spotting them, checking them, and flipping the script.

HOW IT WORKS

Learning to recognize cognitive distortions can change everything. Cognitive distortions are the unhelpful thoughts (*cognitive* means "thoughts") that make us feel bad, act in ways we later regret, or just generally freak out. They are distorted thoughts; they feel completely real in the moment, but they are a symptom and a direct result of our emotions instead of what's actually going on. They are also common, normal, and universal. Cognitive distortions are just part of being human. What's different, and one of the many cool parts about CBT, is that you can actually learn to recognize them and make changes so these thoughts aren't in charge.

Knowing how to challenge these distorted thoughts can make a big difference in how you handle stress, anxiety, and other emotions. Think of cognitive distortions like a filter on an app that distorts the images—it makes you see things in a way that's not real. In the picture you can kind of see the person behind the dog ears and nose that have suddenly been pasted on, but it's hard to see them clearly. Cognitive distortions are mental filters that twist your view or perspective and make it seem different (usually worse) than what's really going on. The distortions feed off your insecurities and fears to make situations look more negative or just generally worse than they really are.

Cognitive distortions are often also negative automatic thoughts. The difference is that negative automatic thoughts are more spontaneous, while cognitive distortions specifically twist reality in negative ways. Cognitive distortions fall into specific categories that you can learn to recognize. By identifying these categories, you can start to see when your mind is distorting reality and pinpoint the specific ways your thinking might be skewed. As a result, you will start to see patterns in your thinking.

STRATEGY: DECODE DISTORTIONS AND EXPOSE THOUGHT TRICKS

So, how can you fight back against these distortions? The first step is becoming aware of them. Once you know what to look for, you can start challenging these distorted thoughts by asking yourself whether they're true or just your mind playing tricks on you. The goal here isn't to become overly optimistic, but to see things in a more balanced and helpful way (you may notice a pattern here). Cognitive distortions are universal, but knowing about them, recognizing them, and catching them is a skill. This is your chance to make some real changes.

Catastrophizing: The Very Worst Situation

Ever find yourself assuming the worst possible outcome in any situation? Like if you bomb a test, you become convinced you'll never graduate? That's called *catastrophizing*. In the moment you feel terrible, and that overwhelming emotion makes you see the worst-case scenario. It doesn't help that it feels completely true in the moment.

Example: You text a kid you like, and they don't reply immediately. You start thinking, "That's it, they think I'm a loser. They're screenshotting this and sharing it with everyone right now."

 CATASTROPHIZING

Can you think of an example of a time you catastrophized?

_____

_____

REALITY CHECK

1. **What's the best-case scenario? What's the most likely scenario?** Chances are, neither involves such a big outcome. In reality, things are more often than not in the middle—not always, but often.

_____

_____

_____

2. **How will you feel about this situation in a week, a month, and a year from now?**

_____

_____

3. **Have you been in a similar situation before? What happened then?**

_____

_____

4. **What would you say to a friend who had this thought?**

_____

_____

_____

Overgeneralization: "This ALWAYS Happens"

Ever feel like one mistake means you're bad at everything? _Overgeneralization_ happens when you believe that a single setback defines all your abilities. It's when you take one negative event and apply it broadly to your entire life.

Example: _You get a C on your math test and think, "I'm terrible at math. I'll never get into a good college."_

EXERCISE OVERGENERALIZATION

When was a time you overgeneralized?

_____

_____

REALITY CHECK

1. Do you use words like "always," "never," "everyone," or "no one"? These words can make you feel like a single mistake defines everything you do. **List the words you tend to use when you overgeneralize.**

_____

_____

_____

2. **What are specific examples that prove your overgeneralization(s) wrong?**

_____

_____

_____

3. Is this really true _all the time_? Chances are, it's not. Remember, one off day doesn't mean every day will be the same. **Think back to the past week: how many days were terrible and how many were pretty good?**

_____

_____

_____

4. What was the context of the mistake? Was it a particularly tough test? A fight with a friend? Were there already-existing stressors at the time?

_____

_____

_____

5. If you share your thoughts with a friend or family member, what are they likely to tell you? It can be helpful to get someone else's take on things. When our perspective gets muddy, trusted people can help us see things a little more clearly.

_____

_____

_____

Black-and-White Thinking: Missing the Gray

Life's rarely all or nothing. If you find yourself thinking you're either a genius or a total idiot with no in between, you're stuck in *black-and-white thinking*. The real world exists in shades of gray. Start recognizing the middle ground. This can be harder than it seems as our brain seems determined to make things feel extreme, but when you start to catch yourself in this thinking error, you can pull yourself out.

Example: *You make a minor mistake in a lacrosse game and think, "I'm terrible at this. I don't know how I made the team."*

EXERCISE BLACK-AND-WHITE THINKING

Describe a time in the last week when you got stuck in black-and-white thinking.

REALITY CHECK

1. **What would you say to a friend in the same situation? Would you tell them to expect the worst? Why or why not? Would it be helpful?** Often (usually?) we are kinder and more rational with others than we are with ourselves.

2. **What is some evidence that your thought is not true?** For example, maybe you made a mistake in the game, but you also made some great plays. One slip-up doesn't define your skill. You're also allowed to have a bad day without that reflecting your overall performance. Take a look at the stats of your favorite professional athlete; their stats are not 100 percent success.

3. **What is the worst-case scenario and the probability it will occur (from 0 to 100 percent)?**

4. **What is an example of a more neutral outcome? What is the probability it will occur (from 0 to 100 percent)?**

_____

5. **What is an example of a more positive outcome? What is the probability it will occur (from 0 to 100 percent)?**

_____

6. **Is the worst-case scenario as likely as it feels?** Often, neutral or positive outcomes are more probable, which can help put your worries into perspective.

_____

Personalization: It's All About Me

Do you always feel like it's "your fault" when something goes wrong? If so, it's likely due to _personalization_. It's exhausting and unfair to carry the weight of the world on your shoulders. Part of learning to manage this distortion is distinguishing between what's your responsibility and what's not.

Example: You were assigned to organize a group project, but one team member didn't complete their part on time. The project didn't turn out as planned, and you assume it's entirely your fault for not managing the group better.

EXERCISE PERSONALIZATION

When was a time you made it "all about you"?

_____

_____

REALITY CHECK

1. **What are some past experiences where you personalized situations? How many of those were actually "all about you," and how many turned out not to be about you at all?**

    _____

    _____

    _____

2. **What is really in your control?**

IN MY CONTROL (WHAT I HAVE THE POWER TO CHANGE)	OUT OF MY CONTROL (WHAT I CAN'T CHANGE)

Why did you act the way you did? What were your intentions? Recognize that you can't control others' actions or reactions, only your own.

_____

_____

_____

3. **If you were an outsider looking at the situation, what would you tell someone if they were in your shoes?**

_____

_____

_____

Should Statements: Shoulda, Coulda, Woulda

Have you noticed yourself thinking, "I should know exactly what I want to do in the future" or "I should be able to handle everything on my own"? *Should statements* are another type of cognitive distortion. In this type of thinking trap, our thoughts make us believe we have to be perfect to be successful. In reality, when we put this kind of strict pressure on ourselves, we get more perfectionistic. And, when we get perfectionistic, we are less flexible and less successful.

Example: You think, "I should be getting straight A's, I should be super popular, and I should be a starter for the varsity team."

EXERCISE SHOULD STATEMENTS

Describe a time you found yourself thinking of what you "should" do.

_____

_____

REALITY CHECK

1. **Instead of telling yourself what you "should" do, focus on what you "can" do at this moment.** This shifts you from dwelling on what are sometimes unrealistic expectations to actively engaging with what you're ready and able to do right now. Doing something is better than doing nothing, and you are more likely to avoid the task if you feel incapable of doing it.

"SHOULD" STATEMENTS	➡	"CAN" STATEMENTS
I should be able to solve this problem.	➡	I can focus on this problem right now.
	➡	
	➡	
	➡	

2. What is success, really? Do you see success as either achieving beyond your wildest dreams or being a complete failure? Challenge your definition of success. Can you redefine success to include personal growth, learning from mistakes, and enjoying what you do?

_____

_____

_____

3. Break down the "should" into smaller, manageable steps that lead to your goal. For instance, instead of saying "I should be the best player," start with "I want to improve my skills starting with _____ and then moving to _____."

4. Treat yourself with kindness. When you catch a "should" statement, ask yourself whether you would say the same thing to a friend. For example, replace "I should have known better" with "It's okay to make mistakes; I can learn from this."

   Write a kindness statement to yourself:

_____

_____

Emotional Reasoning: Me, Myself, and I

When we feel something in a big way, we are wired to pay attention and take the feeling seriously, and with good reason. Feelings are a crucial source of information for humans. But feelings can also be very misleading. They can make us believe things that aren't true or exaggerate the reality of a situation. It's important to recognize when emotions are driving our thoughts (this is called *emotional reasoning*) and to balance them with facts. By doing this, we can make more rational and balanced decisions.

Here's how it might look: You have a big test coming up and you feel extremely anxious. Your feelings might tell you, "I'm going to fail this test because I feel so nervous." However, if you look at the facts, you might see that you've studied hard, done well on past tests, and understand the material. Recognizing this emotional reasoning can help you respond to situations more calmly and realistically.

Example: You feel nervous before a presentation and think, "I feel anxious, so I will definitely mess up this speech."

 **EXERCISE** EMOTIONAL REASONING

Can you think of a time you listened to misleading feelings?

REALITY CHECK

1. Set aside a ten-minute block each day, preferably not right before bed, just for worrying. During this time, write down all your worries and let yourself think about them. If worries pop up during the day, remind yourself that you have dedicated time to address them later. Gently tell yourself, "This isn't the time to worry; I'll handle this

during my worry time." This way, you can keep your worries from taking over your day and stay focused on what you need to do. By scheduling worry time, you can manage your anxieties better and prevent them from overwhelming you.

When will you schedule worry time?

---

2. When you're overwhelmed by a strong emotion, take a moment to pause and ask yourself, "What are my feelings, and what are the facts?" **In the following chart, write down your feelings in one column and the facts in the other. Then, challenge your feelings asking whether there is actual proof.** This helps you see things more clearly and stops your emotions from twisting reality. By separating feelings from facts and looking for evidence, you can make better, more balanced decisions.

FEELINGS	FACTS	IS THERE REAL PROOF FOR THIS FEELING? Y/N
I'm going to mess up my speech to the class.	I got a B+ on my presentation last week. My teacher said she liked my speech outline.	No

Spotlight Effect: All Eyes on Me

When we get anxious or stressed, it can feel like everyone is watching us and judging us. This feeling is another cognitive distortion, and it's called the *spotlight effect*. It happens because we're so worried about being judged that it seems like all eyes are on us. But the truth is, people don't think about us nearly as much as we think they do. Most people are too busy with their own lives to focus on ours. It's called the spotlight effect because it feels like a spotlight is shining on us, making us the center of attention, when, in reality, we're likely the only ones thinking about us at that moment.

Example: You trip in the hallway and think everyone will notice and laugh at you, even though most people probably didn't even notice.

 SPOTLIGHT EFFECT

When have you felt that everyone is watching or judging you?

REALITY CHECK

1. When you start feeling self-conscious, take a moment to pause and ask yourself, "Is anyone really paying as much attention to me as I think they are?" **Think about a recent time when you felt self-conscious and fill in the following chart.**

MY SELF-CONSCIOUS SITUATION	WHAT YOU THINK OTHERS MIGHT HAVE BEEN THINKING OR DOING AT THAT MOMENT	COMPARE THIS SITUATION TO A SIMILAR EXPERIENCE OF YOUR OWN	REALITY CHECK STATEMENT
I tripped in the hallway and felt like everyone was staring at me.	People were probably thinking about their own classes or talking with friends.	When I saw someone trip last week, I barely noticed because I was worried about my math test.	most people are too busy with their own thoughts to focus on me. It's likely they didn't even notice.

2. Shift your thinking away from yourself (this is hard but totally possible) and focus on the person you think is judging you. Ask questions, show interest, and listen actively. This shifts your attention away from yourself and makes you feel less self-conscious. Engaging with others also helps build stronger connections, which can further reduce your anxiety. Plus, when you genuinely focus on others, you might find they are more interested in sharing about themselves than judging you. People generally like others more when they show genuine interest in them.

3. Combat negative thoughts with positive affirmations (that are positive but also true and helpful, not just rainbows and ponies). When you catch yourself thinking negatively, remind yourself of your strengths and achievements. For example, tell yourself, "I'm confident and capable," or "I'm doing my best, and that's enough." **Write these affirmations down and keep them somewhere you can see them daily, like on your mirror or in your notebook.**

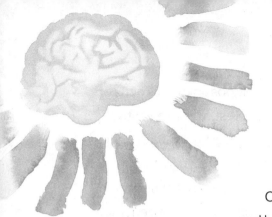

Mind Reading: Predicting

We often think we know what other people think about us, but in reality, unless we're psychic, we usually get it wrong. Our brains tend to assume the worst about what others think and how the future will unfold. Anxiety and stress make us feel like we need to know these things, and they work hard to convince us that these feelings and thoughts are true. But just because something feels true doesn't mean it is. It's important to remember that what you imagine others are thinking is often not the reality.

Example: You post a photo on social media and then worry, "Everyone will think I'm trying too hard."

 **EXERCISE** MIND READING

Can you think of a time you assumed you knew what someone was thinking?

_____

_____

REALITY CHECK

1. Reframe the situation by catching a negative thought and turning it into something more positive and realistic. Next, challenge it by asking yourself whether it's really true and what proof you have against it. Then, flip it around to something better. **Finally, write down how this new thought makes you feel and how it changes your view.**

NEGATIVE AUTOMATIC THOUGHT	IS IT REALLY TRUE? WHAT PROOF DO YOU HAVE?	BETTER THOUGHT	HOW THE NEW THOUGHT MAKES YOU FEEL
Everyone will think I'm trying too hard.	I don't know what other people are thinking. No one has ever told me I am trying too hard.	I'm sharing a moment where I feel good, and that's what matters.	I feel happy when I look at my photo and remember how much fun I had.

2. Behavioral experiments are one of the best strategies in CBT. To do a behavioral experiment, you test the accuracy of your thoughts by gathering real-world evidence. In this situation, you would post the photo and note the actual responses you get (likes, comments, etc.). Compare these to your initial assumption and note whether your thought was accurate or not. For example, you might find that you received positive feedback and support, which contradicts your negative assumption. Behavioral experiments let you test out your beliefs and see whether they are inflated worries or valid assumptions.

MY THOUGHT	EVIDENCE AND FACTS	WAS MY THOUGHT ACCURATE? Y/N
If I post my photo on social media, no one will comment on it.	Three friends liked my post and one wrote, "Wow! So cool!"	No

Mental Filtering: See What You Want to See

Do you ever find yourself noticing only the bad and filtering out the good? That's called *mental filtering*. It's like getting an A on a test but obsessing over the one question you got wrong and forgetting about all the ones you got right. When you focus only on the negative, you miss out on the bigger picture and all the positive things happening around you.

Example: You score twelve points in a basketball game but your team still loses. You can't stop thinking about that one missed shot, and you tell yourself that you lost the game for the team, forgetting all about the points you scored and the shots you blocked.

When do you filter out the good in life? What have you missed?

REALITY CHECK

1. Gratitude journals can literally change how you see the world. They are a powerful tool for mental filtering. And, they're fun. Here's how to start: Find a notebook or designate a note on your phone specifically for gratitude. Each night, take a few minutes to remember and write down three specific things that went well during your day. Focus on detailed and concrete moments rather than general statements. For example, instead of writing, "I have a great dog," write, "When my dog woke me up this morning, he was smiling and wagging his tail, which made me feel happy and loved," or "I finished my homework earlier than usual and had time to watch my favorite show." This practice not only helps you appreciate the small joys but also trains your brain to look for and remember the positives throughout your day.

   I am grateful for:

2. After any win, take a few minutes to think about your top three standout moments. Close your eyes and replay these moments in your mind like a highlight reel, picturing everything in detail: the looks on people's faces, the sounds around you, and what you were doing. This trick comes from sports psychology and helps athletes focus on their best moments to boost confidence and motivation. By regularly visualizing your highlights, you're building a mental collection of your best achievements. This keeps you positive, reminds you of what you're capable of, and helps you appreciate your successes even more.

My three standout moments:

_____

_____

_____

Labeling: Don't Let One Thing Define You

Labeling yourself based on a single event is another type of cognitive distortion. When you label, you limit how you see yourself. Instead of seeing the full picture, your perspective shrinks and narrows, causing you to miss out on seeing yourself (or others) in their totality. It's important to challenge these labels and remember that one event doesn't define who you are. You're a complex person with many strengths and weaknesses—you are not one thing or the other.

Example: _You break your curfew and your parents catch you. They are so mad, and you feel terrible. You say to yourself, "I am such a bad kid."_

 **EXERCISE** LABELING

What labels have you given yourself? How do they limit you?

_____

_____

REALITY CHECK

1. Create a vision board: a poster or bulletin board filled with pictures, quotes, and thoughts that help you fight off negative labels. Print or cut out images that inspire you, quotes that boost your confidence, and thoughts that challenge the negative thoughts. You could include photos of favorite moments; this could be a big thing like winning a game or a simple thing like hanging out with family. The only rule is that it makes you feel like you are more than just a label: you are important. You might also want to include some coping thoughts like, "One setback doesn't define me" or "I am more than my mistakes" or whatever makes you feel motivated. Arrange everything on a poster or corkboard and put it somewhere you'll see it every day, like your bedroom wall or your locker. Seeing these reminders daily will help you focus on your positive qualities and goals, especially when you're tempted to label yourself negatively. This vision board should remind you that no single event defines you; you're a unique person with so many awesome qualities and abilities.

    Things I want to include on my vision board:

    _____

    _____

    _____

Quotes for my vision board:

_____

_____

_____

2. Create a timeline of awesomeness: using a regular piece of paper turned long ways, draw a long horizontal line. This line represents your timeline from your earliest memory to now. Along this timeline, mark all the awesome things you've accomplished and the positive experiences that stand out: when you felt proud, capable, or just good about yourself. These don't have to be the biggest achievements, although they can be; they just have to be experiences where you felt valued and valuable. Write a brief description of each event on the timeline. Sometimes we can change our perceptions (confront the labels) by seeing a visual reality that differs from the labels we create for ourselves. This is a different way of looking at the idea of "facts vs. feelings": just because a label feels true doesn't mean it is. It's important to challenge one-dimensional views of yourself and see the bigger picture—the complex person you really are.

Things I want to include on my timeline:

_____

_____

_____

_____

_____

REFLECTIONS

REFLECTIONS

- **Cognitive distortions are mental filters that warp reality.** They twist your perception and make things seem bigger and worse than they actually are. But you now know all of their tricks, and by catching them you have the ability to stop them from taking over and making everything seem bigger and more terrible than it really is.

- **Everyone experiences cognitive distortions—it's part of being human.** But now you have the knowledge and strategies to handle them. Whether it's catastrophizing, overgeneralization, or any other distortion, you can now recognize these tricks your mind plays. The goal isn't to become overly positive but to see things in a balanced and helpful way. Keep practicing these techniques, and over time, you'll find yourself feeling more secure, confident, and in control. Keep this guide handy, revisit these strategies often, and before long those distortions won't stand a chance! You've got this!

CHAPTER 3
HIT THE PAUSE BUTTON

Mindfulness 101

Alex, a fifteen-year-old high school sophomore, felt like his mind was always racing. He couldn't stop thinking or worrying; schoolwork, exams, family, friends—all of it was constantly racing through his mind. Alex's thoughts were all tangled up; each thought was pressing for his attention and everything felt like the most important thing. Alex hated feeling this way; he felt like he was never "in the moment" or able to relax and just enjoy.

Alex went to a school lecture on mindfulness. He went without expecting much, but as he listened, something clicked. The speaker talked about mindfulness as a way to slow down racing thoughts and just be in the moment. It wasn't about fixing everything; it was about accepting things as they are, including his own feelings. Alex had never imagined himself the mindful type, but this just made sense. He decided to give it a try.

As Alex started practicing mindfulness, things began to change. He learned to pause and breathe when he felt overwhelmed, to notice his thoughts without getting lost in them. Over time, he found that he could concentrate better, not just on his homework but also with friends, family, and in most situations. His stress didn't just magically disappear, but Alex felt like he was able to handle challenges. He learned to steady his thoughts and clear his mind, one breath at a time, and he felt so much better than before.

Mindfulness is when you intentionally notice your thoughts, feelings, and what's happening around you without judging yourself. It's about being present and really paying attention. When you're mindful, you realize that good and bad thoughts and feelings come and go. You aren't defined by your thoughts and feelings—you are always you.

HOW IT WORKS

When you practice mindfulness, you train your brain to slow down and be less reactive and more in the moment. Mindfulness helps you become more aware of your thoughts and feelings without getting tangled up in them. You learn where you can pause, catch yourself, and pull yourself back into the moment and, as a result, see things more clearly. By doing this, you make better and more thoughtful choices about how you react to things that happen around you. Life becomes less about being right or wrong, and more about just being a part of the experience.

Mindfulness also helps you have more control over your emotions by teaching you to notice feelings and acknowledge them without letting them overwhelm you. Noticing your thoughts and feelings as they come and go helps you realize that they're just passing events in your mind. They don't define you. Learning to observe your thoughts as separate from yourself lets you see them more objectively. You are more than your thoughts. The key to mindfulness (as with most things) is practice. The more you do it, the more you use it.

STRATEGY: TAKE FIVE

Life can get pretty hectic and overwhelming, and it's easy to put off practicing mindfulness. "Take Five" is a quick and effective way to ground yourself and bring your focus back to the present moment. It only takes a few minutes, and you can do it anywhere.

1. Find a comfortable and quiet spot where you can relax without interruptions. You can sit on a chair, on the floor, or anywhere you feel comfortable. Next, if you feel comfortable, close your eyes (if you feel comfortable) and take three deep breaths: inhale slowly through your nose while counting to four. As you breathe in, let your chest and belly expand. Exhale slowly through your mouth to the count of six. Feel

yourself relaxing more with each breath. When you feel ready, begin to engage your senses, one at a time.

2. **FIVE THINGS YOU CAN SEE:** Open your eyes and quietly name five things you can see around you. Try to pick items you usually wouldn't notice and make sure you notice specific things—the blue dots on the floor tile, the red color of the clock face, the shiny silver of metal on the chair.

3. **FOUR THINGS YOU CAN TOUCH:** Reach out and touch four objects within your space. This might mean feeling the texture of your clothing, noting the softness, scratchiness, warmth, cold, etc.; the surface you're sitting on and whether it's soft, hard, smooth, or bumpy; the bracelet on your wrist; the softness of your hair; the tip of your fingernail—anything is fine. Pay attention to the sensations of touching the item. Describe the texture, temperature, and other physical qualities of each object.

4. **THREE THINGS YOU CAN HEAR:** Listen carefully and identify three sounds you can hear. These could be distant noises or sounds close by. This could be traffic, the hum of an appliance, or birds chirping outside.

5. **TWO THINGS YOU CAN SMELL:** Next comes smell, and it can be a little harder to do this if you are in a public space. You might subtly smell your hand and notice the lingering scent of hand soap, sniff your sleeve and notice the laundry smell or other scents, and, if it's long enough, smell your hair and the shampoo scent.

6. **ONE THING YOU CAN TASTE:** It could be the aftertaste of a meal, a piece of gum, or simply the freshness of water. If you can't taste anything in the moment, remember a specific taste, such as cinnamon, chocolate, or something you like that has a strong flavor.

7. Once you've gone through all your senses, close your eyes again and take a few more deep breaths. Think about how you felt during the activity. Did you notice anything new? How do you feel right now? Take a minute to reflect to help solidify this new skill in your mind.

_____

_____

_____

EXERCISE TAKE FIVE

List three things that surprised you about this activity.

_____

_____

_____

When are three times in the past week that this practice would have been useful?

_____

_____

_____

This is a super practical activity that lets you practice mindfulness in the moment by shifting your attention to experiencing your immediate surroundings through your senses. It also teaches you to notice details in your environment, which helps calm your mind and brings your focus to the present moment. You can use this exercise pretty much anywhere at any time. If you notice your heart racing with worries, take five. If you feel overwhelmed and unable to get started on a project, take five. You get the idea. ☺

STRATEGY: BREATHING COLORS

For this activity you will need a quiet space to really engage with the process as you focus on breathing and imagery. It's worth a few minutes of your time to truly learn this exercise; it's helpful and kind of lovely.

1. Find a comfortable spot where you can sit or lie down quietly without any distractions. Close your eyes and let yourself sink into your seat and feel fully supported.

2. Take a deep breath in through your nose, counting to four as you inhale. Feel your chest and belly expand as you breathe in. Hold your breath for a count of four and then slowly exhale through your mouth, counting to six as you exhale. Notice the sensation of your breath leaving your body.

3. Continue breathing deeply and slowly, imagining each inhalation as a vibrant color entering your body. Make sure you choose a color that represents a positive emotion or feeling for you. It could be calming blue, soothing green, or energizing yellow.

4. Each time that you exhale, visualize any negative emotions or tension leaving your body as a different color (this color can be one with less positive connotations). In your head, tell yourself that you are releasing the stress or worry each time you breathe out. You might say to yourself, "With this exhalation, I am releasing stress and tension." Visualize the color leaving your body through your breath and dissipating into the air.

5. Continue this breathing exercise for several minutes, focusing on the rhythm of your breath and the colors flowing in and out of your body.

EXERCISE BREATHING COLORS

How did you feel before starting the exercise?

☐ Anger   ☐ Anxiety   ☐ Confusion   ☐ Fear

☐ Frustration   ☐ Guilt   ☐ Sadness   ☐ Stress

As you practiced breathing in colors, how did your internal experience shift?

_____

_____

_____

As you exhaled colors, actively releasing stress and tension, what did you notice in your body?

_____

_____

_____

What are three insights or lessons you gained from this mindfulness practice that you'd like to remember for next time?

_____

_____

STRATEGY: TAKE A (MINDFUL) WALK

Mindful walking is an ancient practice; it's a form of meditation that has been used in many cultures and spiritual traditions. In Buddhism, walking meditation is used to cultivate awareness and presence. In indigenous cultures around the world, walking the land is often a form of prayer or a way to connect with the earth. Mindful walking allows a deep connection with the environment and an appreciation of the moment. In today's Western culture, mindful walking is increasingly popular as a way to bring calm and peace into daily life. Ready to give it a try?

1. First, find a safe place to walk. If possible, choose an area with natural beauty. This can mean anything from a stroll past fields in a country setting to a walk down busy streets with trees and window boxes.

2. When you start walking, go at a slow, relaxed pace. This isn't about getting exercise or reaching a destination quickly. It's about observing and experiencing the world around you. You have a natural walking speed; try to turn down the speed by just a little bit so you recognize this as different from your normal walks.

3. Engage your senses (are you noticing how often senses come up in mindfulness?):

   - **SIGHT:** Notice the colors and movements of things around you. Observe the shapes of leaves, the patterns on tree bark, or the way shadows move on the ground. Try to see the details you usually overlook. As you pay attention, you will notice new things you haven't seen before.

   - **SOUND:** Listen to the sounds that are all around. Can you hear birds chirping, leaves rustling, people talking, or distant traffic? Pay attention to how the sounds change as you move.

   - **SMELL:** Take in the scents around you. If you're lucky, you can smell flowers, freshly cut grass, or the crispness of the air after rain. But even in city settings, there are smells you can notice—the scents from a food truck, the smell of steam coming up from a grate, or the aroma of coffee from the person walking next to you. Notice how the smells shift as you walk through different areas.

- **TOUCH:** If it's safe to do so, touch objects you pass. Feel the texture of a leaf, the roughness of tree bark, or the smoothness of a rock. Notice whether it feels cool, cold, warm, or hot.

- **TASTE:** Theoretically you would taste a berry from a garden, but that likely isn't the best idea. Instead, think about how a fresh berry would taste in your mouth. Let yourself imagine the burst of flavor, the warmth of the berry, and the taste of sweetness.

4. Every few minutes, stop walking, stand still, and (if safe) close your eyes. Take a deep breath and focus on what you've observed. As you breathe in, let yourself fill up with emotion. Notice how you feel in your body and mind.

5. When your walk is almost over, take a moment to consciously focus on feeling grateful for the time you spent walking, engaging, and observing. Offer thanks to the world for the beauty that you just experienced.

Date of walk: _____

Location: _____

The questions below can be completed outside on a park bench at the end of your walk or at home on a cozy couch, wherever you feel the most comfortable.

SENSORY EXPLORATION

VISUAL OBSERVATIONS	
What is one specific thing I noticed?	
What feelings came up as I observed this thing?	
When I paid attention to this detail, what thoughts or feelings came up?	

AUDITORY DISCOVERIES

What sounds did I hear?	
What thoughts or feelings came up while listening?	
How did the sound influence my mood or thoughts?	

SCENT EXPERIENCE

What is a smell I noticed?	
What memories, thoughts, or feelings did the smell trigger?	
What did I notice about myself from this reaction?	

SENSATION OF TOUCH	
What textures did I feel?	
What emotional or physical reaction did I have to the touch?	
In what ways did touch impact my experience?	

TASTE (REAL OR IMAGINED)	
What did I taste (real or imagined)?	
What feelings or thoughts came up related to this taste?	

REFLECTIVE INSIGHTS

What were my thoughts and sensations during pauses? What did I discover about my internal experience (thoughts, feelings, bodily sensations) when I stood still?

_____

_____

_____

Record three specific moments of gratitude from the walk.

_____

_____

_____

BROADER CONNECTIONS

How can the act of slowing down and observing help me in my daily life?

_____

_____

_____

How does the environment around me affect my inner world? How can I carry this awareness with me?

_____

_____

_____

Where and when are some other places/times that I can use this mindfulness?

How do I feel now at the end of my walk compared to when I began?

REFLECTIONS

REFLECTIONS

- **Mindfulness isn't about silencing thoughts or emotions but instead recognizing and accepting them as part of the human experience.** Mindfulness teaches us that our thoughts and feelings are like weather—they pass over and change, but the sky always remains. When we step back and realize that we are the sky and not the weather, we get a sense of ourselves as so much more than our momentary thoughts and emotions. We also gain a perspective that lets us stop judging our thoughts and feelings so harshly. There is more to life than this temporary distress, and we don't have to believe everything we think.

- **Mindfulness encourages us to turn regular moments into opportunities for presence and awareness.** With mindfulness, we can approach life with curiosity and compassion. Mindfulness is less about doing and more about being. It's a commitment to living fully in the present. It's the practice of embracing life, the good and the bad, without judgment. This moment, right now, is enough, and you are enough.

CHAPTER 4
FROM MEH TO YEAH

The Power of Behavioral Activation

Meet Catherine, a seventeen-year-old high-school junior who often finds herself overwhelmed and so tired that she just wants to lie down. She doesn't want to do anything—not even her favorite activities. She feels stuck, her energy is sapped, and the easiest tasks seem overwhelming. Catherine hates feeling this way but she also feels unable to change.

Catherine learns about behavioral activation (BA), a technique that involves doing things you love to improve your mood—even when they are the last thing that you want to do. At first she thinks this sounds too simple and even a bit ridiculous. When her mood is low, the last thing she wants to do is get up and start doing the activities she usually enjoys. But she is feeling so bad that she decides to give it a try. She doesn't have anything to lose and is so ready to feel better.

She starts with small things, like drawing, listening to her favorite music, and hanging out with friends for shorter periods of time. At first it feels forced and it takes a great deal of effort to make herself participate in the activities. But, over time, she gradually begins to notice a difference. Each activity brings a small boost to her mood.

She realizes that it's not just finishing the task but the action itself that kick-starts a positive shift in mood. When she starts moving, whether it's doing an activity she used to enjoy, getting some exercise, or hanging out with friends, her mood lifts, and she feels better. It's all about getting in motion to start feeling those good feelings again. The more she engages in these activities, the easier it becomes, and this creates a positive cycle of action and improved mood.

Catherine learns that BA isn't just about making yourself do the things you used to think were fun; rather, it's about taking real steps to break the cycle of feeling down. This helps her see that even when she's feeling low, she has the power to make choices that can lift her mood.

"Act the way you want to feel" is another way of defining *behavioral activation*. In BA, you challenge yourself to break out of a slump by doing things you usually enjoy, even if they seem like too much in the moment. Making this change, to do the thing that will make you feel better, often feels awkward or forced at first. That makes sense, but it also is temporary. The more you push yourself to "act the way you want to feel" the easier and more natural it feels. Positive change starts with BA, and it's okay to start small. The more you practice, the easier it gets, and the better you will feel.

HOW IT WORKS

When we're feeling down, most of us find ourselves withdrawing from people, getting lost in endless scrolling, or bingeing TV shows. The couch becomes a refuge, and the thought of going out, even to do things you love, feels overwhelming. Chores and homework? They are just not going to happen.

It's common to feel like you don't want to do anything when your mood is low, and sometimes you do need to let yourself relax and recharge, but if you let that feeling take over, you often end up feeling even worse. It might seem like a good idea to watch six hours of TV, but most of us feel irritable and unproductive at the end. This creates a loop where not feeling energetic leads to not doing activities, and avoiding activities keeps your energy low. The key to breaking this cycle is to make a big effort to do something that you would have enjoyed if your mood weren't low.

How Low Mood is (Unconsciously) Perpetuated

This is where behavioral activation helps. BA pushes you to do activities that matter to you or that you like, no matter how you're feeling right now. The idea is straightforward: by doing something that has made you feel good in the past, you can start to shift your mood. It's definitely challenging, but it truly does make a difference.

Studies have found that BA works for treating depression.[1][2] The core idea is that avoiding activities, especially ones you enjoy or find meaningful, can make your mood worse and deepen feelings of sadness. On the other hand, getting back into these activities can lift your mood and improve your mental well-being. So, getting involved in things that matter to you is more than just helpful—it's a proven way to boost your overall mental health and happiness.

---

1 Ekers, D., L. Webster, A. Van Straten, P. Cuijpers, D. Richards, and S. Gilbody. 2014. "Behavioural Activation for Depression; An Update of Meta-Analysis of Effectiveness and Sub Group Analysis." PLOS One 9(6): e100100.
2 Wang, X., and Z. Feng. 2022. "A Narrative Review of Empirical Literature of Behavioral Activation Treatment for Depression." *Frontiers in Psychiatry* 13: 845138.

STRATEGY: RECONNECT AND RECHARGE

Doing things that make you feel accomplished or happy kicks off a new and energizing cycle: you do something enjoyable, which lifts your mood, and then you're more likely to keep doing enjoyable things. It takes some effort to reconnect with the activities and people you used to enjoy, but it is a real way to fight sluggishness that can drag you down when you're not feeling great. In the end, it recharges you.

The process starts with taking action, despite the strong desire to isolate and check out. You probably know this already, but the anticipation of an activity is usually the worst part. Once you get moving, you most likely enjoy the experience and wonder why it was so difficult to get started. Taking action against the tiredness and drain that come with low mood can be tough. But you can create change, and it does get better.

This strategy helps you reconnect with activities that boost your mood and energy. By reflecting on what you used to enjoy and rating how much energy these activities give you, you can find the best ways to get started on activating your mood and your energy.

EXERCISE RECONNECT AND RECHARGE

1. **Think of activities you enjoy or used to enjoy but haven't done in a while.** This can literally be anything: baking cookies, petting your dog, sketching, or turning up the volume on your favorite music and singing along. Write these activities down in the chart below.

2. **Next to each activity, jot down some quick notes about what you used to enjoy about it.** What made it fun or satisfying for you?

ACTIVITY	WHAT I REMEMBER LIKING ABOUT IT	ENERGY BOOST RATING 1-5
Walking my dog, Stevie	It made Stevie so happy. Her tail would wag like crazy, and she would jump up and down when I got her leash out. She would look back at me on the walk with the happiest face.	5, lots of energy

3. Of all the activities you listed, which one (or ones) seem the most possible, the most enjoyable, and the most energy-giving to you right now?

_____

_____

4. What are all the reasons to do the activity, and what are the reasons not to? **Use the following chart to list the pros and cons.**

ACTIVITY: WALK STEVIE	REASONS TO DO IT	REASONS NOT TO DO IT
	Stevie really loves it.	I'm tired.
	I enjoy being outside.	I don't know how I'll feel after.
ACTIVITY:		
ACTIVITY:		

Reflect on your experience. What did you discover? Are there more reasons to do the activity or more reasons not to? If there are more reasons not to do it, take a closer look. If the reasons feel valid, move on to the next best activity and try the list again until you find some activities you're willing to do.

_____

_____

_____

_____

STRATEGY: MAKE THE TIME

Now that you've identified some activities to boost your mood, you need to add them to your schedule to make sure you actually do them. Behavioral activation works by tricking your brain into feeling better by acting like you're feeling better. "Act the way you want to feel" is another way to think about BA. But, as you already know, this is easier said than done.

The first step is to schedule your chosen activities into your day. Because low mood usually makes us want to hide away under the covers, we need a concrete plan for our time to show our brain that we are really going to do this. This means having a written plan for the day, and including some of the behavioral activation activities in the day.

 MAKE TIME

Use the schedule below to make a rough plan for the upcoming week.

DAY	TIME	ACTIVITY
monday	5:00 p.m.	walk Stevie

STRATEGY: TRACK YOUR PROGRESS

Keeping track of the activities you do and how they affect your mood is a key part of behavioral activation. Sometimes, when you're feeling low, it seems like nothing can lift your spirits. That's why it's helpful to actually note down what you do and how you feel afterward. This is a way to gather real evidence of what's boosting your mood and what's not. Your brain most likely will try to trick you into believing that nothing helps, and you need more objective data to outsmart your mood.

The first step is to add activities that you enjoy to your daily routine. Then, note how you feel and any thoughts you have before, during, and after each activity. This can show you the kind of thoughts that come up with different activities and how they might be influencing your mood. Over time, this record can reveal patterns, like which activities consistently make you feel better, and help you understand the connection between what you do, what you think, and how you feel.

Before you get started, take a look at Catherine's daily activity chart to give you an idea of how it works. As you can see, she identified the activities she enjoys: walking her dog Stevie, talking with her best friend on the phone, and playing guitar. She also listed studying for her math test because she had a goal to do well on it but hadn't actually been putting in the time to study.

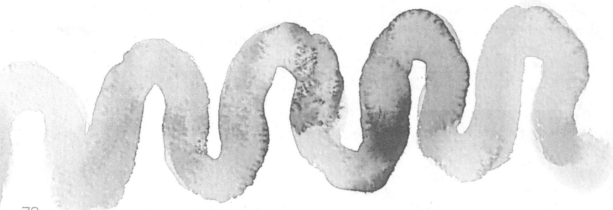

DAY AND TIME	ACTIVITY	MOOD BEFORE (1–10)	THOUGHTS BEFORE	MOOD DURING (1–10)	THOUGHTS DURING	MOOD AFTER (1–10)	THOUGHTS AFTER
monday 7 a.m.	Walking Stevie	4	"I really don't want to do this."	6	"Stevie is the best!"	7	"I'm glad I did that."
Tuesday 4 p.m.	Call Sarah	5	"Do I even have anything to talk about?"	7	"I missed this."	8	"That was fun."
Wednesday 4 p.m.	Study for math test	3	"I can't focus; it's useless."	5	"making progress, slowly."	6	"Okay, it wasn't a total waste."
Thursday 7 p.m.	Play guitar	6	"I'm out of practice; I don't know what to do."	8	"This isn't as bad as I thought."	9	"I'm really happy I did this."

Catherine found that by the end of the week, her mood was actually a little better.

EXERCISE TRACK YOUR PROGRESS

Use the chart below to fill in your activities, moods, and thoughts when using behavioral activation.

DAY AND TIME	ACTIVITY	MOOD BEFORE (1–10)	THOUGHTS BEFORE	MOOD DURING (1–10)	THOUGHTS DURING	MOOD AFTER (1 10)	THOUGHTS AFTER

Behavioral activation is one of most effective CBT strategies, and it really is a great tool when you're struggling with low mood. Just like Catherine found her way back to feeling better by pushing herself to participate in activities, you can also learn to push through and do the things you enjoy. Be prepared to feel skeptical or even frustrated by this activity at first; that's normal. Feel the feeling and do it anyway.

REFLECTIONS
REFLECTIONS

- **Challenge yourself.** Behavioral activation is all about challenging yourself to do something—even when every fiber of your being wants to stay in your comfort zone. Now that you've seen the power of the intervention, the next step is about keeping it going. Consistency is key: doing the activity even when you don't feel like it, *especially* when you don't feel like it. This is the hardest part. Take a deep breath, count to five, or find a mantra you tell yourself. The more you do it, the better things get.

- **Create a new normal.** As you continue with behavioral activation, remember that it's about creating a new normal for yourself—one where action is a part of your daily life. The more you engage in activities you enjoy, the better they feel. Pretty soon you may notice that the activities you once had to push yourself to do become the ones you look forward to the most.

- **The true power of BA unfolds over time.** It's not just about the immediate lift in mood you might experience after doing something enjoyable or fulfilling. It's about the cumulative effect of regular engagement in life, even when it feels tough to get started. This repeated practice can lead to lasting changes in your mood and behavior, making you feel better and better. Every step is progress, and progress, no matter how slow, means that you are moving forward.

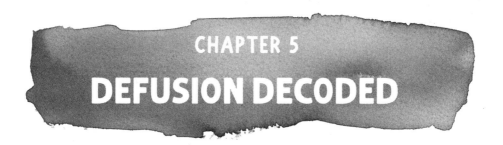

CHAPTER 5

DEFUSION DECODED

Untangling from Sticky Thoughts

Sophia, a sixteen-year-old high schooler, used to feel like the smartest person in the room. But lately, things have changed. Now it seems like everyone is doing better than her, knows more, and gets higher scores than her. Sophia has always been critical of herself and gets stuck on her faults, both real and imagined, and it is only getting worse as the work gets harder. The more she thinks about how much she is struggling, the more her negative automatic thoughts (NATs) sound like:

"It never used to be this way."

"I peaked early and this is as good as it gets."

"I guess I am just not as smart as I thought I was."

These thoughts make her feel terrible. She repeats these thoughts so often in her head that her brain truly believes them. The more the NATs take over, the more worried she becomes that she won't get into a good college or have a good future. "I am literally stupid" and "I have no future" are constant thoughts ringing through her head. Her confidence is low and her motivation is slipping.

Sophia wants to make these thoughts less powerful and less overwhelming. She is learning a technique called defusion, which is part of acceptance and commitment therapy (ACT). Defusion is a skill that helps her step back from her thoughts and see them as they are—just thoughts—rather than continue to feel and believe that they are real and true.

Defusion is a technique that helps you change how you interact with your thoughts and emotions. Instead of getting stuck in negative thoughts, you learn to observe them, almost step outside of them, so that they can't control you.

Defusion draws from Buddhist practices that focus on mindfulness and nonattachment to thoughts. One of the main ideas of Buddhism is that attachment to thoughts and feelings can lead to suffering. By recognizing that thoughts are just thoughts, not the reality itself, you can reduce your internal struggle. Defusion allows you to encounter thoughts with a sense of curiosity and detachment, which allows you to respond—not react—to each thought.

Practicing defusion is kind of like learning to watch clouds drift across the sky without having to chase after them: they just move across the sky and you observe them without judging, blaming, or pursuing them. In this practice, thoughts are just thoughts; they aren't necessarily true and they don't define who you are. Defusion is a way to step outside the intensity of your thoughts and see them as something that you experience rather than something that defines you. Over time, this practice helps reduce the power of your thoughts and makes them feel less overwhelming and less urgent.

HOW IT WORKS

Defusion works by:

1. Creating distance: Step back from negative thoughts and be more mindful.

2. Taking thoughts less seriously: See unhelpful thoughts as just "words in your head."

3. Focusing on experiences: Stay present and pay attention to your feelings and surroundings.

4. Developing flexibility: Identify unhelpful thoughts and practice not getting caught up in them.

When Sophia uses defusion, she practices rephrasing her self-criticism from "I'm stupid" to "I'm having the thought that I'm stupid." This doesn't sound like much, but the change in language creates a distance between herself and her negative thoughts.

By realizing that her thoughts aren't facts, Sophia starts to separate herself from the negativity, making those thoughts feel less intense and overwhelming. Instead of getting caught up in the constant negative messages, she recognizes them, tells her brain "thanks for looking out for me," and then lets them go.

Sophia is beginning to understand that she has the power to respond to her NATs in a way that's helpful and constructive, rather than harmful. With practice, she's hoping defusion techniques will change her relationship with her thoughts and allow her to focus on her goals with a clearer, more confident mindset.

STRATEGY: ZAPPING THE POWER OF THOUGHTS

Using this strategy, you will repeat a word over and over. Sound exciting? I know, it's weird, but when you repeat a word, you take away some of its power. Your brain unlearns the negativity associated with the word through overuse—you essentially neutralize it through overdoing it. The more you repeat something, the less meaning, weight, and negativity it holds.

1. Think of a word that carries a lot of emotional weight for you. It could be a word that you feel describes you negatively, like "weird," "failure," or "fat."

2. Find a comfortable, private space where you can speak out loud without being interrupted. This is one of those activities that you definitely want to do in a place where people can't overhear you.

3. Say the word out loud repeatedly, as quickly as you can while still pronouncing it clearly. Keep going for at least one full minute.

4. Notice how the word begins to lose its meaning. It may start to sound strange or just become a series of sounds.

5. After you've finished, take a moment to write about your experience.

How did the emotional power of the word change during the exercise?

_____

_____

_____

How did you feel about the word before and after the exercise?

_____

_____

_____

How will you remember this exercise and the feeling of distance the next time this word or thought comes up in a negative way?

_____

_____

_____

To make this really take hold, you will need to practice every day for a few weeks to truly see the difference, but it only takes a few minutes a day and is totally worth it. By repeating a word again and again, you turn a heavy, emotional word into just a sound, taking away all the judgment and self-criticism attached to it. The power this word or thought has over you becomes smaller and smaller until it is nothing more than a string of letters that have no impact on your mood or emotions.

STRATEGY: THOUGHT PARADE

This strategy invites you to be an observer of your own mind, like watching a parade from the sidewalk. You'll see your thoughts just as they are—like floats passing by—not part of your core self. This strategy strengthens your ability to defuse, which means you learn how to watch your thoughts and feelings without letting them take over. It's about learning to take a step back mentally. This skill teaches you to be focused on the here and now and helps you handle your emotions without getting overwhelmed by them.

1. You will need five to ten minutes for this practice. Find a quiet and comfortable space where you can relax without anyone interrupting you. Sit or lie down, whichever feels more comfortable, and close your eyes. Take a few slow, deep breaths in through your nose and out through your mouth. Feel your muscles start to relax and your heart and your breathing slow. Tell yourself, inside your head, that you are calm and relaxed. Repeat inside your head: "I am calm and relaxed."

2. Imagine yourself sitting on the curb of a busy parade route. It's a beautiful, sunny day, and you came here to watch the Thought Parade. Notice your environment, what you see, how you feel, take note of your senses, and notice that you feel safe and comfortable in this space.

3. Now, picture each of your thoughts as a colorful float in the parade. Every float is different and each float represents one of your thoughts. You can tell the thought represented by the message or image on the float. Just watch the parade go by without focusing on any specific thought-float.

4. Next, change your focus by pulling it inward, toward your thoughts. Start to observe your thoughts as they occur in your mind. Begin to imagine your thoughts as specific floats passing by in the parade. Some might be bright and colorful while others may be soft and calming. The images can look however you want them to look, and it's okay if they don't exactly mirror the specific thought—the float just needs to represent the thought in some way that makes sense to you.

5. As a thought-float approaches, acknowledge its presence, but don't try to change it in any way. You are simply a spectator watching this parade go by, and your only job right now is observing the floats pass.

6. If a thought-float starts to feel a little stuck or you notice strong emotions, gently remind yourself that it's just a thought passing by in the parade. Let your mind distance you from the thought-float by seeing it as something separate from you. You are simply noticing the thought-float as it passes by.

7. Continue to watch the parade of thoughts, allowing them to come and go without judgment or attachment. If your mind becomes quiet and no thoughts are passing by, that's okay too.

8. After the exercise, take a moment to reflect on your experience.

 **EXERCISE** THOUGHT PARADE

Which thought-floats stood out or were the most memorable?

_____

_____

_____

What patterns or themes did you notice among your thoughts?

_____

_____

_____

How did it feel to observe your thoughts without getting caught up in them?

Was it difficult to stay a passive observer, or did it come easily? What did you notice about being an observer?

How can you bring this practice into your daily life when dealing with intrusive or distressing thoughts?

Remember that just like a parade, thoughts come and go. You have the power to choose which ones you listen to and engage with and which ones you simply let pass by. This exercise is a good tool for practicing cognitive defusion and gaining more control and distance from your thoughts.

STRATEGY: TURN DOWN THE VOLUME

This strategy teaches you how to decrease the impact of your thoughts by changing how you respond to them. Imagine your thoughts have a volume knob, and you now have the ability to lower the volume on your thoughts. As you get better at this, you can reduce distracting thoughts to tiny whispers, and focus instead on what's happening right now.

1. Just like with the previous exercises, start by finding a quiet space where you feel safe and comfortable. Get super comfy—you can sit or lie down, whatever feels best to you. Close your eyes and take a few deep breaths to center yourself. Pay attention to your breath as it enters and leaves your body. Breathe slowly in through your nose and even more slowly out through your mouth.

2. Next, visualize a radio. This can be a music app on your phone, the car radio, or kitchen speakers—any image that conveys the idea of a radio works. The radio you are imagining represents the inner noise of your mind: the thoughts that won't stop and the noise that is too loud.

3. Now, imagine you can control the radio's volume. You can choose whether to turn the volume up or down, change the type of music, or even turn it off completely.

4. Think of a negative or self-critical thought that often gets in the way and causes you to feel bad about yourself. Imagine that this thought is currently playing on your radio. You can hear it blasting out of the speakers. It is so loud that you want to cover your ears and leave the room.

5. In your mind, tell yourself that you have control over the volume of this thought. Visualize turning down the volume on this thought and notice it getting quieter and quieter. You can turn it down to a whisper or even mute it entirely. Experiment with different volumes to see how it changes. Remember to visualize yourself changing the volume settings; this helps your brain learn and adapt more effectively. Imagine lifting your hands from your ears and note the relief your body feels when the noise is turned down.

6. If the negative thought continues to interfere with your thinking, then change the station. Once again, visualize yourself changing the station, selecting a new playlist, or searching up your favorite artist. Now, actively bring to mind a positive or neutral thought, such as a favorite song, a happy memory, or a calming mantra, instead of the negative automatic thought.

7. After the exercise, take a moment to reflect on your experience.

EXERCISE TURN DOWN THE VOLUME

Describe how it felt to have control over the volume and even the content of your thoughts as you turned down the volume or switched the station.

_____

_____

_____

Notice what feels different in your body, your mind, and your emotions. **Write down what you notice.**

_____

_____

_____

Whenever you encounter negative thoughts, remember that you have the power to adjust the volume or even change the station. This is a tool that is always available to you. Set a reminder on your phone or leave a sticky note out to remind you to practice this technique daily. With consistent practice, this technique will become a natural part of your routine, helping you maintain a clearer, more focused, and much calmer mind.

REFLECTIONS
REFLECTIONS

- **Defusion is a powerful tool for handling negative thoughts.** It means taking a step back and seeing your thoughts as they are: temporary and impersonal. Your thoughts do not define you. Defusion helps you put distance between yourself and your negative thoughts.

- **When you practice observing your thoughts without getting swept up in them, you start to realize they are just part of your experience, not your entire identity.** This new viewpoint can make your thoughts feel less intense and overwhelming. The strategies you learned in this chapter are ways to make your thoughts less powerful and overwhelming. Keep practicing these techniques—the more you practice, the more effective they become.

- **By stepping back and viewing your thoughts as just passing events, you gain a clearer perspective.** This separation allows you to understand that your thoughts are not you. Over time, this practice will reduce the intensity of the negative thoughts and make them feel less overwhelming. The more you practice defusion, the easier it gets.

CHAPTER 6

EMERGENCY BRAKES

Mastering Distress Tolerance

Maria is fifteen, and she loves Taylor Swift, making jewelry, and volunteering at the animal shelter. Maria is a person who feels things deeply, and she sometimes gets completely overwhelmed by her emotions. When Maria gets overwhelmed, she often gets mad at other people, overreacts to not-that-terrible situations, and does things that she later regrets.

When Maria gets angry or feels taken advantage of, she usually feels a strong urge to deal with the situation right then, in that moment. As you can probably guess, when she reacts in a moment of high anger, she usually doesn't act the way she wants or get the response that she wants. She wants to be able to handle her emotions better, and she is ready to learn.

Distress tolerance is a series of tools within dialectical behavior therapy (DBT). The tools are not meant to fix the situation; rather, they are designed to help you lower your level of distress to get through the experience without making it worse. The skills used in distress tolerance are ways to help in the immediate moment; they are short-term assistance, not a long-term solution, but sometimes that's exactly what is needed.

Self-awareness is the main idea in distress tolerance, and the first step Maria takes in learning these techniques is to start to recognize cues from her body and mind that alert her to stress and overwhelm. Once she realizes what's happening, she starts to practice her skills. Distress tolerance skills are often sensory (involving the five senses). For example, she might smell an essential oil, listen to music, splash icy cold water on her face, or do thirty jumping jacks (or some other type of short-term but intense physical exercise). These distress tolerance skills help pull her out of overwhelming emotions and regain emotional balance without overreacting or taking it out on someone else.

Maria decides to make distress tolerance her main strategy for handling overwhelming emotions. After using the skill for a while, she realizes it keeps her centered. She's tired of pretending her feelings don't exist or acting like everything's okay when it isn't: that doesn't work. Now, Maria is learning to recognize the early signals that she's reaching her emotional limits and can put her skills to work.

HOW IT WORKS

Distress tolerance skills target uncomfortable feelings and situations. Distress tolerance work is not about solving the problem, but about surviving and tolerating the tough moment without adding extra pain or making impulsive decisions that lead to regret. In other words, the goal is to get through situations where your emotions are out of control without making things worse. By recognizing these signs early, you can take steps to manage your emotions before they become too intense. This self-awareness lets you use strategies to calm down and approach situations with more openness and less reactivity.

PHYSICAL SENSATIONS: Your body gives signals when your stress level increases. You might feel your heart pounding, or notice your stomach feeling queasy or nauseous, or become aware of a dry feeling in your mouth. These are all physical symptoms of stress, but we all can feel stress differently in our bodies. If you can learn to notice these physical sensations before they get overwhelming, you can step in and make changes to manage your stress before it becomes too big.

THOUGHTS: Your thoughts are another way to spot stress. Remember negative automatic thoughts (NATs)? These NATs tend to show up in a big way during times of stress. Everyone's thoughts are unique, but some of the more common stress-related thoughts involve feeling like you're being unfairly blamed or targeted, that things are out of control, or that you can't do everything that you are expected to do. You might notice feeling helpless ("I can't handle this") or isolated/separate/different from others ("No one understands me"). Catching and checking these thoughts early helps you change them before they gain power and take over.

BEHAVIORS: If you catch yourself clenching your fists, snapping at friends and family for no real reason, consistently overreacting to situations that aren't really that big of a deal, or pulling away from friends, it could mean you are going through a high-stress period. Stress puts our body on edge and makes us more reactive to small things. Paying attention to your behaviors means you are more likely to catch your stress before it gets too big.

STRATEGY: SPOTTING DISTRESS

This technique is all about helping you catch and handle stress before it becomes too much. The sooner you notice the signs, the easier it is to stay in control. Self-awareness is key, and this exercise teaches you how to practice and develop your self-awareness skills.

The exercise below is meant to be practiced frequently. Start by using it at least once a day, ideally when you feel stressed. It's okay to do this after the event has passed, just fill it in as you think you experienced it. Your answers don't have to be exact or perfect.

Date: _____

Time: _____

1. **PHYSICAL SENSATIONS:** What are you feeling in your body right now? Is your heart beating faster than usual? Is your stomach queasy or jumpy? Is your mouth dry?

SENSATION	DESCRIPTION (WHAT YOU FEEL)	INTENSITY (LOW, MEDIUM, HIGH)

2. **THOUGHTS:** What negative automatic thoughts are you having in this moment? Do you feel targeted or that something is unfair? Are you feeling helpless or thinking, "I can't handle this"? Do you feel isolated or like no one understands you?

THOUGHT	DESCRIPTION (WHAT YOU THINK)	HOW OFTEN DO YOU HAVE THIS THOUGHT (OCCASIONALLY, FREQUENTLY, OR CONSTANTLY)?

3. **BEHAVIORS:** How are you acting in the moment? Are you holding tension in your shoulders? Clenching your fists? Snapping at people or overreacting to small issues? Are you withdrawing from friends?

BEHAVIOR	DESCRIPTION (WHAT YOU DO)	HOW OFTEN DO YOU DO THIS (OCCASIONALLY, FREQUENTLY, OR CONSTANTLY)?

4. **Take a moment to reflect on what you've observed.** Recognizing these signs early can help you use strategies to manage your emotions effectively.

_____

_____

_____

_____

STRATEGY: THE ACCEPTS METHOD (SURFING YOUR EMOTIONS)

The ACCEPTS Method is a set of coping techniques for keeping your head above water. To use a surfing metaphor, ACCEPTS lets you ride the waves of emotion rather than getting pulled under and wiping out. But you don't just ride waves effortlessly; surfing is seriously difficult. It requires balance, patience, and skill, and learning to manage your feelings uses a similar skill set.

Any distress tolerance skill will be about riding the waves, not fighting them, and this is true for the ACCEPTS method. The idea is to stay on top of the emotion, feel it, be aware of it, and use skill, strength, and balance to stay afloat. Each letter in ACCEPTS is a step that helps you stabilize and balance when your emotions overwhelm you.

Over the next week, find a time to try each technique and record your experiences on the following worksheet. Here is what the acronym of ACCEPTS stands for.

A—Activities

What It Does: Distracts you with positive activities.

How to Use It: Choose activities that absorb your attention and are positive. This helps shift your focus from stress to something enjoyable, but it needs to be something super engaging.

Example: Create a playlist of songs that always get you moving, start a new level on your favorite video game, or bake your favorite cookies.

C—Contributing

What It Does: Helps you by helping others.

How to Use It: Do something nice for someone else. This gets you out of your head and adds a splash of good vibes.

Example: Compliment your mom (seriously) on something she did well recently, send a text to a friend to just check in on them, or help a sibling or friend with a challenging task.

C—Comparisons

What It Does: Puts things in perspective.

How to Use It: Think about past challenges you've faced and gotten through successfully. Remember that you have been through worse and made it. This perspective shift can make your own problems seem less overwhelming.

Example: Remember when you literally climbed a mountain on a hike. You didn't think you could do it, but you kept pushing and felt so proud when you made it to the top.

E–Emotions

What It Does: Shifts your emotional gears.

How to Use It: Change your emotions so that they are more positive or calming. This can help turn down the intensity of the tough stuff.

Example: *If you're feeling down, watch some short videos that are truly funny, dance to your favorite high-energy song, or do fifteen jumping jacks (right now—go!).*

P–Pushing Away

What It Does: Gives you a break from the heaviness, stress, or anxiety.

How to Use It: Set your worries aside for now. Imagine putting them in a box on a shelf. You'll deal with them later when you're ready.

Example: *When thoughts about tomorrow's exam won't stop popping up as you're lying in bed trying to sleep, give yourself permission to put off worrying until after breakfast tomorrow. Setting a specific time lets your brain and worries know that you aren't blowing it off—you will attend to it—just not right at this moment.*

T–Thoughts

What It Does: Reroutes your thought train.

How to Use It: Change the channel in your mind. Get absorbed in something that requires focus and keeps the tough thoughts at bay.

Example: *Try reciting the lyrics to your favorite song without looking, counting all the blue items in the room, or doing math problems in your head.*

S—Sensations

What It Does: Soothes you through your senses.

How to Use It: Find comfort in things you can touch, taste, smell, see, or hear. This can calm you down by engaging your senses in a positive way.

Example: Squeeze a stress ball, sip a cold drink or warm tea, or snuggle under a soft blanket.

 THE ACCEPTS METHOD

A—ACTIVITIES

Date: _____

Time: _____

Activity: _____

Time spent: _____

How did it help? What did you notice?

_____

_____

_____

_____

C-CONTRIBUTING

Date: _____

Time: _____

Contribution: _____

Whom did you help?: _____

What was your mood after?

_____

_____

C-COMPARISONS

Date: _____

Time: _____

Current challenge: _____

Past win or someone else's challenge: _____

What is your new perspective?

_____

_____

_____

E—EMOTIONS

Date: _____

Time: _____

Tough emotion: _____

Activity that shifts it: _____

What new emotions did you find?

_____

_____

_____

P—PUSHING AWAY

Date: _____

Time: _____

Worry: _____

How you pushed it away: _____

When you'll come back to it: _____

T—THOUGHTS

Date: _____

Time: _____

Stressful thought: _____

Thought redirection activity: _____

What was your focus level?

_____

_____

S—SENSATIONS

Date: _____

Time: _____

Stressful thought: _____

_____

Sensory comfort: _____

How did your perspective change?

_____

_____

STRATEGY: YOUR DISTRESS TOLERANCE KIT

This strategy is about solidifying the skills you've learned in this chapter, and to do so you are going to make an actual distress tolerance kit. This kit will be full of tangible things and reminders that help you navigate through big emotions.

1. Find a container that feels personal and comforting to you. It could be a small box, a pouch, or even a designated pocket in your backpack that only you know about. You want this container to be something small enough that you can keep it close to you when you need it.

2. Gather your supplies:

    -   **REMINDER TO BREATHE:** Choose something that you can hold in your hand or wear (like jewelry) and touch when you are practicing your breathing techniques. This can be whatever you like, but here are some ideas: a small smooth stone that you can hold in your hand or a ring you can turn on your finger.

    -   **WORDS THAT HELP:** Write down the quotes that make you feel better, inspire or motivate you, or just resonate with you. These might be lines from songs, books, movies, or really anything. Maria carried lines from her favorite Taylor Swift song, and she read them over and over when she needed help.

    -   **MINDFULNESS AWARENESS:** Mindfulness is an enormously helpful practice that works when we remember to use it. Remembering is always the trickiest part. Many teens find it helpful to wear their watch or bracelet on a different hand as a memory tool. When they automatically look to see the watch, they have to remember it's on the other hand. You can tie this cue to remembering to be mindful. A bracelet works in a similar way, and especially one with strings on the end. When you find yourself mindlessly playing with the string, it can be a cue to switch to mindfulness.

- **SOMETHING BEAUTIFUL (BUT NOT VALUABLE):** Having an item of beauty in your container can remind you to express yourself, look at your thoughts, or look into this moment. Some kids use shells, beads, or even pebbles that appeal to them.

- **COPING CARDS:** Remember all of the coping thoughts that you've worked on? They can flit right out of your mind when you get overwhelmed. Having an index card with the coping thoughts that help you the most can be enormously useful.

- **STRATEGY CARDS:** Even just writing 5-4-3-2-1 can be enough to remind you to practice grounding. You can add other images or words to remind you of the other tools that work best for you. If you spend some time on the card, it becomes better locked into your memory, and you are more likely to be able to visualize it mentally if you can't get to the actual card. In other words, time spent making it is time well spent.

- **JOURNAL PROMPT CARDS:** Writing almost always helps, but when we're flooded with emotions we can get a little stuck. "What do I write?" is a frequent question. You can make some prompts on a card that are simple and direct: "What am I feeling right now? Where and how am I experiencing the feelings in my body?" or "What is going on around me, right now, in this moment? What do I see, smell, feel, touch, and taste?"

This kit is meant to be uniquely yours and as such there is no right or wrong way to do it. The key is that it helps you feel prepared and equipped to handle big emotions. How it looks and what it contains is as unique as you are. Use the following worksheet to plan your kit.

EXERCISE YOUR DISTRESS TOLERANCE KIT

What container will you use?

_____

- **REMINDER TO BREATHE:** _____

_____

- **WORDS THAT HELP:** _____

_____

- **MINDFULNESS AWARENESS:** _____

_____

- **SOMETHING BEAUTIFUL (BUT NOT VALUABLE):** _____

_____

- **COPING CARDS:** _____

_____

- **STRATEGY CARDS:** _____

_____

- **JOURNAL PROMPT CARDS:** _____

_____

REFLECTIONS
REFLECTIONS

- **Distress tolerance is not one single skill, but rather a group of skills to help manage intense emotions.** When you practice distress tolerance, you are tuning in to catch feelings of being overwhelmed before they get too big, and you're responding with strategies to help the situation from getting bigger and worse.

- **The strategies you've learned can help you navigate difficult feelings.** When you practice these techniques, you build greater emotional resilience and learn to handle tough situations more effectively. Keep these skills handy, and use them whenever you feel overwhelmed.

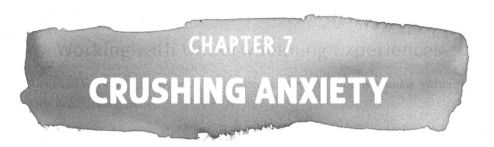

CHAPTER 7
CRUSHING ANXIETY

Regaining Control

Simone, age seventeen, has been called a "worrier" by just about every person in her life for as long as she can remember. Anxiety is a constant for Simone, and there is rarely a part of the day where her thoughts aren't racing to the worst-case scenario or a deeply held fear. She is always replaying conversations in her head and she frequently gets stuck in negative thoughts. Simone feels like she is always on edge, constantly waiting for something else to go wrong. It's a hard way to live, and she is so sick of it.

Anxiety is such a difficult and uncomfortable experience, and it's one of the most common mental health struggles people face. If you've dealt with anxiety, you know how much room it takes up in your mind and you know the pain of always having to worry. Unfortunately, people who don't experience anxiety may not get it or may even unintentionally downplay your experience by telling you to "get over it," "move on," or "calm down," or even get annoyed and tell you to "just stop." It feels terrible when people react like that, and it can make an already tough situation feel even worse.

Anxiety is powerful, and even when we know a thought or feeling isn't true, anxiety can exaggerate the feelings so much that it's hard to believe anything but the feeling. Simone's anxiety makes her think that things are much more likely to go wrong than they actually are. Her anxiety also causes her to forget how strong and capable she really is. In cognitive behavioral therapy (CBT), we refer to anxiety as "an overestimation of risk and an underestimation of resources." In other words, anxiety makes us think situations are bigger and worse than they really are and that you don't have what it takes to deal with it. Here's the truth: feelings aren't facts. Just because something feels true doesn't mean it is. This chapter teaches you how to push back and regain control when anxiety tries to take over.

HOW IT WORKS

Anxiety often causes our minds to jump to conclusions without real evidence. We can know something isn't true in our rational minds, but it still feels true. It's hard not to believe the feelings, and when we do, we often end up in a pattern of negative and fear-based thinking that just isn't true. Cognitive behavioral therapy (CBT) is all about learning to see situations more clearly and accurately, to see the facts despite the feelings. Once you learn to recognize when your brain is spinning out anxious thoughts, you can catch them and question them. You can learn to ask yourself whether they're really true or whether your anxiety is exaggerating and making things seem bigger and worse than they really are. This process teaches you to see when your anxiety is manipulating your feelings and lets you take back control.

Anxiety also tricks you into thinking you can't do things that are uncomfortable or scary, and it tries to get you to avoid situations that make you uncomfortable, even when you know you're perfectly safe. In the moment, it often feels like a good idea to avoid the difficult situation, but that actually increases your anxiety. The more you avoid what you fear, the more you teach your brain that avoidance is the only way. This creates a cycle of fear and avoidance that limits your life and makes your world get smaller and smaller. The strategies you're about to learn will help you break those patterns and face situations with a clearer and more accurate perspective.

Coping thoughts are a simple yet powerful tool for managing anxiety. They're positive, realistic things you can tell yourself when your anxiety tries to convince you that everything is going wrong. Not every coping thought works for everyone, so it's important to try out different ones to find what feels right for you. My go-to coping thought is "this is temporary—it will pass," but some teens I've worked with don't find that thought useful. They have to experiment with a few different thoughts until they find something that really helps them. It's worth taking the time to figure out what works because a good coping thought can be a game-changer when anxiety kicks in.

The key to using coping thoughts is practicing them before you're anxious. Just like you wouldn't try to learn a tough math problem in the middle of a panic, you shouldn't wait until you're anxious to practice coping thoughts. The goal is to get so familiar with them when you're calm that they automatically pop into your mind when things get stressful.

STRATEGY: COPING THOUGHTS

Here are some examples of coping thoughts:

"Just because it feels true, doesn't mean it is true. Anxiety lies and makes things seem bigger and worse than they really are."

"Feelings are temporary. This feeling will end."

"Anxiety is uncomfortable, but I can tolerate discomfort. I have [insert a time you did something uncomfortable and got through it]."

"I am stronger than I feel in this moment. My anxiety is trying to make me believe that I can't do this, but I have done it before, and I can do it now."

"This is just a thought, not a fact. Anxiety thoughts amplify fears. What are the facts in this situation?"

What thoughts would work for you? Some may resonate more than others, and it's important to find the coping thoughts that feel right to you. You know yourself best, and you know what will be the most helpful. There are a lot of ways to choose a coping thought, but many teens find it helpful to remember a time they got through a tough experience successfully and use that as a reminder of their strength. Another common option is to focus on the facts of the situation: "Just because this feels true doesn't mean it is true. The facts are _____."

EXERCISE COPING THOUGHTS

List your coping thoughts:

_____

_____

_____

_____

_____

_____

_____

Now, you get to memorize them. I like to write my coping thoughts on small cards I can carry in my pocket and pull out to practice whenever I have a minute. Most teens I know prefer to write them in a notes app or text them to themselves. The key is to have them close at hand and remember to practice them. Coping thoughts only work if you remember to use them.

Coping thoughts are a super helpful and always accessible tool to help you manage anxiety. They are a strong counter to the anxious feelings that exaggerate the risks and downplay your strengths. Remember, these thoughts are only effective when they are so familiar that they're easy to remember, even during stressful times.

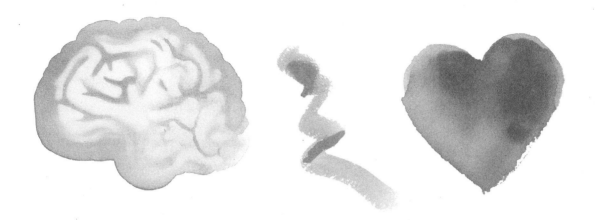

STRATEGY: FACT VS. FEELING

In the midst of anxiety, it can be tough to distinguish between what you know (facts) and what you feel (anxiety). The ability to name the facts and feelings is a fundamental part of managing worries. There is even research that shows that when you simply name the anxiety you reduce your anxious response.

EXERCISE FACT VS. FEELING

1. Think of a recent situation that made you feel anxious. **Write a brief description of the event in the chart.** Remember, no detail is too small if it matters to you.

2. **List your fears, the anxious thoughts that you had in the moment, and the anxious thoughts that occurred later about the situation.**

3. **List the facts.** Detail only the verifiable facts about the event. Remember, facts are things that are true, observable, and can be verified by others.

SITUATION	FEARS	FACTS
I walked by a table during lunch, and I think I heard someone laugh.	They are all laughing at me. They think I am weird, stupid, awkward, or something bad. I am definitely a loser, and people are always judging me behind my back.	One person definitely laughed. I do not know why they were laughing. It may or may not have been at me. In that moment, there was no clear reason someone would laugh at me.

Examine the fears and facts side by side. How do your fears support the facts?

Factually, I don't know why they were laughing. I assumed it was about me without evidence, and it felt that way. In truth, they could have been laughing about me but they also could have been laughing about something else.

How do the facts support your fears?

I don't have any evidence that they were laughing at me. I wasn't doing anything weird or awkward (at least at that moment) and no one was looking at me. And, it wasn't the whole group laughing, it was just one person. My anxiety made it seem like they were all laughing at me, but I don't have any real facts to back that up. Whew.

What is the takeaway here? Reflect on this exercise in the space below.

STRATEGY: EXTERNALIZE THE ANXIETY

This strategy helps you separate yourself from your anxiety and see you and your anxiety as two very different things. YOU are wonderful. You do not want to have anxiety, you did not choose to have anxiety, and it is not your fault that you have anxiety. This technique may seem goofy, but it is super helpful. Give it a chance and see how it works.

EXERCISE EXTERNALIZE THE ANXIETY

1. Give your anxiety a name that reflects its character. Do not use the name of your beloved pet, your best friend, or anyone you love. Give it a name that reflects the actual anxiety. Some names I have heard before are Vex, Morpheus, Snare, and others I can't actually include in this book. **What is your anxiety's name?**

   _____

2. **Draw or write a description of your anxiety as if it were a character in a story.** What does it look like? How does it behave? What are its habits? It doesn't need to be a human; it can be an animal, a monster, a mythological creature, or whatever fits your anxiety best and works for you. Feel free to really get into it.

   _____

   _____

   _____

   _____

   _____

3. This part is probably best done privately. You are going to have a conversation with your anxiety and ask it questions to better understand it. Many people do this through writing in a journal; others switch chairs as they go from themselves to their anxiety. However you want to do it is the right way to do it. **Some questions you might want to ask are:**

    ● Why are you here and bothering me?

    ● What is driving you and giving you energy?

    ● What makes you feel calm?

    ● What do I most need to know about you?

    ● Other: _____

    ● Other: _____

    ● Other: _____

4. **Write a letter.** You will never mail this and no one ever has to see it. Take the information you have learned and the thoughts and feelings you experience to write a letter to your anxiety about the impact it has on your life. Write this as though your anxiety were the character you have chosen and address it using the name you chose earlier. Write deeply and from the heart. It is fine to shred the letter when you're done, but let yourself deeply experience the pain, the frustration, the anger, and whatever else you feel in this letter.

    _____

    _____

    _____

    _____

_____

_____

_____

_____

_____

This activity is not about trivializing or belittling your anxiety but about understanding and externalizing it—taking it outside yourself. By seeing anxiety as an external thing, you don't have to keep blaming yourself or feeling ashamed. You aren't your anxiety. You never have been, and this technique is all about making that crystal clear.

STRATEGY: THE THREE QUESTIONS

Even after you separate feelings from facts and have a conversation with your anxiety, there will still be times that you find yourself anxious. This is a very simple strategy that you can have ready. You simply ask yourself three questions about whatever you're worried about:

1. What is the worst thing that could happen?

2. How likely is that thing to happen?

3. If it happened, how would you cope?

Once you can see the worst-case scenario (and imagine how you would handle it), you might find it isn't as bad as it seemed. Remember, the goal is not to invalidate your feelings, but to see them in the context of reality, reducing the hold anxiety can have on your perception of the world.

1. What's the absolute worst thing that could happen?

2. On a scale of 0 to 100 percent, how likely is that to happen?

3. How would you cope if it happened? What would you do? How would you handle it?

REFLECTIONS
REFLECTIONS

- **The techniques you've learned in this chapter are proven to help manage anxiety.** The strategies teach you to look at situations based on hard facts, not just anxious feelings.

- **Practice these strategies daily.** Write down what makes you anxious and then look back to see what the actual situation was (the facts) versus what you felt. As you get the hang of it, you'll start to see the difference between the reality and your anxiety more clearly, helping you respond to things as they are.

CHAPTER 8
COURAGE QUEST

Exposure Therapy Basics

Meet Jamie, a sixteen-year-old who loves video games and playing soccer. He's a solid student, but his fears are holding him back from doing all of the things he wants to do. Jamie gets seriously anxious about raising his hand in class, he literally feels like he is shaking when speaking in front of the class, and he dreads the idea of being judged or making a mistake. These worries hold him back. He wants to be more confident and take part in class discussions, but his anxiety is constantly convincing him he will screw it up or embarrass himself. It's frustrating because he knows he has good ideas, but his fear seems to always get in the way.

Jamie learns about something called exposure therapy from his school counselor, and she explains it as a way to face his fears slowly, one step at a time. She describes a process where you rate your fears from hardest to easiest and start with the easiest fears. Even that sounds terrifying, but Jamie decides to give it a try anyway.

He starts small—practicing raising his hand in class when he is sure he knows the answer, and slowly building up his confidence. Then, he practices at home in front of a mirror and with his family. He continues to build up his courage by participating in small study groups and gradually raises his hand to ask simple questions in class. It's uncomfortable, but he keeps going through the discomfort and slowly starts to challenge his fears and build confidence.

Jamie puts in the work. He knows that exposure therapy only works when you keep pushing and practicing. Over time, he sees that it really is working. He isn't completely free of worries, but he also isn't so overwhelmed that he doesn't try. Once he gets pretty comfortable speaking up in class, he realizes that he can use this technique in other areas where he feels anxious. He begins to take on small leadership roles in group projects, something he would never have done before. As his confidence grows, he volunteers for bigger responsibilities, eventually leading a school club.

Jamie also uses exposure therapy to get better at asking for help and taking risks. At first, he sticks to asking simple questions, and as time goes on, he feels more comfortable reaching out for support with tougher subjects from teachers and classmates. When it comes to trying out for the soccer team, he is really nervous at first. But after practicing with his friends, he builds up the confidence he needs to give tryouts a shot.

Social situations that once felt intimidating are now easier for Jamie. He knows that if he wants to be comfortable with groups of kids, he needs to start small. He gets a friend to go to a football game with him, and their plan is to leave at halftime, but they end up having so much fun they stay through the game.

Jamie thinks of exposure work kind of like training for a marathon (even though he hasn't actually faced that challenge yet). He knows that if he wants to run twenty-six miles someday, he has to be constantly pushing and slowly adding miles. It's the same with exposure work. Once he reaches a place where he feels comfortable, he adds a little bit of a challenge to the situation to keep working at it. Jamie has learned that by taking manageable steps and facing his anxiety directly he is able to push through his worries and accomplish what he sets out to do.

Exposure therapy is a powerful CBT tool for overcoming fears and anxieties. It works by gradually helping you face the things that scare you in a safe and controlled way. This technique can be used for many different situations that you might avoid because they cause you stress. These can be specific anxiety situations like social anxiety, fear of public speaking, or a phobia (a specific fear of something like dogs or bees). But exposure therapy can also be used as a tool to build bravery; even if something isn't causing you overwhelming anxiety, if your worry is causing you to avoid the thing you want to do, exposure therapy can help.

HOW IT WORKS

Exposure therapy helps you face your fears little by little, making them less scary over time. When you practice doing exposures, you teach your brain to unlearn the fear. When we avoid something, our brain thinks it is too much or too big to face. The next time we face that scary thing, our brain remembers the fear and tries to get us to escape it. Exposure is about unlearning that fear response and letting our brain know that this really is not as bad as it feels.

The idea behind exposure is based on something called habituation. You may have learned about this idea in science class. Basically, the more you're exposed to something, the less impact it has on you. A classic example of this is with a swimming pool. Have you ever jumped into a pool in spring before the water has really had a chance to warm up? You jump in and it's freezing! If you get right out, you feel better, but the water will still be freezing when you try again. If you want to get past the discomfort of the cold water, you have to tough it out and stay in the pool until your body gets used to the temperature. Over time, you feel more and more comfortable, and it's not because the water temperature is changing: it's because you have habituated to the temperature. It's the same with your fears—the more you face them, the less power they have.

Avoidance, on the other hand, is when you stay away from things that make you anxious. One of the most annoying parts about avoidance is how natural and easy it is. When we feel scared and avoid the fear, we immediately feel better. Unfortunately, the good feeling doesn't last. What feels like a relief in the moment of avoiding actually ends up making your anxiety bigger. Your brain learns that whatever you feared really was so big and scary that you had to try to escape it. Your brain starts to believe that the situation is too much for you to handle. In cognitive behavioral therapy (CBT), avoidance is a problem and exposure is the solution. Avoiding stops you from learning that you can cope with the anxiety but exposure helps you learn that you are able to do hard things.

Avoidance is especially tough when it comes to anxiety because it creates a cycle that makes your fear grow. When you avoid something, you might feel better for a bit, but that temporary relief makes you more likely to keep avoiding similar situations. Over time, avoidance makes your anxiety worse and limits your experiences. You miss out on opportunities that you would actually enjoy. Avoidance also prevents you from getting used to the feared situation. Usually, facing something scary over and over makes it less frightening. But if you keep avoiding it, your brain continues to see it as a threat, keeping your anxiety high.

As you practice exposure therapy, you probably will find that the things you fear (and then likely avoid because of the fear) follow a similar pattern. At first, the idea of starting a conversation or standing up to speak in front of a class might feel terrifying. But as you start with smaller tasks—like saying hello to a classmate or talking in front of a mirror—and then gradually work up to more challenging ones, you'll notice the fear lessens. Your brain is learning that these situations aren't as threatening as they seemed. This method helps you understand that you have the strength to face more than you give yourself credit for, moving step by step toward mastering your fears.

STRATEGY: EXPOSURE

Here are the basic steps of exposure therapy:

1. **IDENTIFY YOUR FEAR:** Clearly identify what you are afraid of or avoiding because it causes discomfort. This could be anything from speaking in front of a class to posting online.

2. **CREATE A FEAR LADDER:** Make a list of activities related to your fear, ordered from least scary to most scary. This helps you break down the fear into manageable steps.

3. **START SMALL AND PLAN YOUR STEPS:** Begin with the least scary activity on your fear ladder.

4. **GRADUAL EXPOSURE:** Gradually work your way up the ladder, exposing yourself to more challenging activities. The key is to take small, manageable steps.

5. **STAY CALM AND TOLERATE THE DISCOMFORT:** Practice staying calm during each exposure. Focus on your breathing and remind yourself that you are safe. The coping thoughts you practiced in the previous chapter will be helpful here.

6. **REPEAT, CLIMB, PROGRESS:** Repeat each step until it becomes less scary. Then, move on to the next step on your ladder.

Start by clearly identifying what you are afraid of. This could be a specific situation, an object, or an activity that causes you anxiety or discomfort.

How does this fear affect your daily life?

Are there specific situations or triggers that make this fear worse?

What thoughts and feelings come up when you think about this fear?

How do you currently cope with or avoid this fear?

EXERCISE CREATE A FEAR LADDER

Creating a fear ladder (also known as an exposure hierarchy) gives you a road map to face your fears step by step. You always start with the easiest steps at the bottom and slowly, at your own pace, work your way up to the harder ones at the top.

Break down your fear into smaller, more manageable steps, starting with the least scary activities and gradually moving to the most challenging ones. **Start by listing every possible step you can think of, big or small, that may be helpful to facing the fear.**

Rate each step in terms of how scary it feels on a scale of 1 to 10, with 1 being the least scary and 10 being the most scary.

EXERCISE START SMALL AND PLAN YOUR STEPS

BEFORE COMPLETING THE STEP

When and where will you attempt the step?

_____

_____

What can you do to make yourself feel more comfortable and prepared?

_____

_____

Who can support you as you take this step?

_____

_____

How will you reward yourself for completing this step?

_____

_____

AFTER COMPLETING THE STEP

How did you feel before, during, and after the activity?

_____

_____

What thoughts and feelings came up during the activity?

_____

_____

What helped you stay calm and focused?

_____

_____

What was challenging about this step?

_____

_____

What did you learn from this experience?

_____

_____

How will you apply what you learned to the next step on your ladder?

_____

_____

Repeat this worksheet for every step on your fear ladder.

EXERCISE REPEAT, CLIMB AND PROGRESS

How will you know when you're ready to move to the next step?

What can you do if you feel stuck or overwhelmed?

How will you celebrate your progress along the way?

How can you keep track of your progress and stay motivated?

By following these steps and answering these questions, you should have a clear exposure hierarchy complete with tools, skills, and strategies to help you climb high. The fear ladder is a key part of doing any exposure work; it guides you to success in a thoughtful and realistic way. Your ladder should help you gradually face your fears, unlearn your fear response, build confidence and resilience, and use the coping skills you've learned. Remember, the goal is to take small, manageable steps and celebrate each success.

STRATEGY: AVOIDING AVOIDANCE

Avoidance plays a significant role in anxiety, and yet, avoidance is the first thing we want to do when confronted with a scary or uncomfortable situation. But, when you avoid situations that make you anxious, you actually end up reinforcing your fears, making them stronger over time. Avoidance prevents you from facing your fears and discovering that you can handle the discomfort; the avoidance cycle keeps you stuck in your fears.

This strategy guides you through identifying your avoidance behaviors and developing ways to tackle them. By working through the steps, you will learn to challenge negative thoughts, build effective coping strategies, and gradually expose yourself to the situations you avoid.

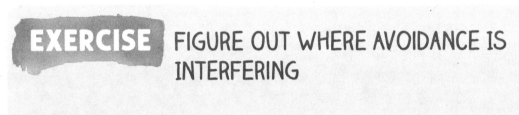 **EXERCISE** FIGURE OUT WHERE AVOIDANCE IS INTERFERING

What specific situations or activities do you avoid because of fear or anxiety?

_____

_____

_____

_____

_____

What physical sensations or emotions do you experience when you think about these situations? This might be a knot in your stomach or the feeling of dread or fear when you consider the situation.

_____

_____

_____

_____

_____

List at least three situations or activities you avoid. Describe why you avoid them and how this avoidance affects your life.

_____

_____

_____

How would your life be different if you didn't avoid these situations?

_____

_____

_____

EXERCISE UNDERSTAND THE IMPACT OF AVOIDANCE

Think of a situation that recently occurred that caused anxiety and where, instead of facing the anxiety, you avoided it (no judgement! This is normal!). **Take yourself back in time and watch and notice how it played out.**

_____

_____

_____

_____

_____

What immediate benefits did you gain from avoiding this situation?

_____

_____

_____

How will your goals and your life be affected if you continue to avoid this? Describe what it will look like in one month.

_____

_____

_____

Describe what it will look like in one year.

_____

_____

_____

How does avoidance affect your self-esteem and confidence?

_____

_____

_____

What specific negative automatic thoughts (NATs) do you have about the situations you avoid?

_____

_____

_____

How realistic are these thoughts? Are they based on facts or assumptions?

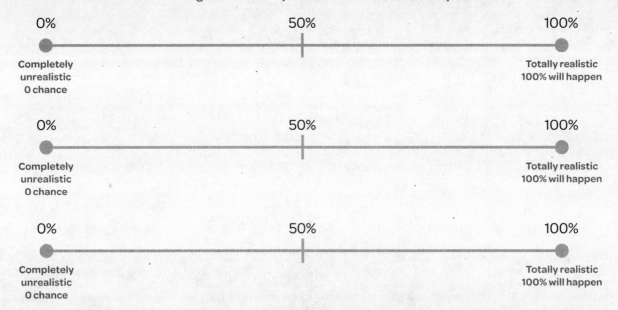

What evidence do you have that supports and that contradicts these negative thoughts?

EVIDENCE THAT SUPPORTS THE NAT	EVIDENCE THAT CONTRADICTS THE NAT

STRATEGY: COPING STRATEGIES

Think of this as creating your personal playbook for handling stress and anxiety. You'll have the chance to explore various techniques and figure out which ones work best for you when it comes to avoiding avoidance and doing the exposure.

BOX BREATHING: Sit comfortably and close your eyes. Inhale slowly through your nose for a count of four, feeling your lungs fill up. Hold your breath for another count of four. Then, exhale slowly through your mouth for a count of four. Finally, hold your breath again for a count of four before starting the cycle over. Repeat this process several times until you feel more relaxed and focused. The Navy SEALS use this technique...just saying.

POSITIVE SELF-TALK: Replace NATs with positive coping statements and affirmations, such as "I can handle this" or "I am strong and capable." Remember, don't go overly positive or your brain won't believe it. True and helpful is key.

VISUALIZATION: Where do you feel most at peace? Is it a beach, a forest, or maybe your own room? Picture yourself in this place. What do you see around you? Focus on the details, like the colors, shapes, and objects that make you feel calm.

GROUNDING TECHNIQUES: Focus on your senses to stay present. Describe five things you see, four things you hear, three things you can touch, two things you can smell, and one thing you can taste.

PROGRESSIVE MUSCLE RELAXATION: Sit or lie down in a comfortable position. Starting with your feet, tense the muscles for a few seconds, then slowly relax them. Move up your body, tensing and relaxing each muscle group, until you've worked through all major muscles.

TALK IT OUT: Call or reach out to a trusted person and talk about what's bothering you. Sharing your feelings can help you see things more clearly and feel less alone. A trusted person will listen, support you, and may even offer helpful advice or a different perspective.

MINDFULNESS MEDITATION: Find a quiet place to sit comfortably and close your eyes. Focus on your breathing, noticing each inhale and exhale without trying to change it. If your mind starts to wander, gently bring your attention back to your breath, and continue for a few minutes.

CHOOSE YOUR TOP THREE COPING STRATEGIES

Read through the suggested coping strategies. Think about which ones resonate with you and why and choose your top three. **List those below:**

1. _____

2. _____

3. _____

Think about how you can use the three coping strategies in your daily life. Imagine yourself in different situations where you might feel stressed or overwhelmed, and picture how these strategies can help you cope. **Write down one specific situation for each strategy and describe how you would use it.**

Coping Strategy 1: _____

Situation: _____

Think of a time at school, like before a big test or during a tough class, when this strategy could help you stay calm and focused.

Coping Strategy 2: _____

Situation: _____

Consider a social scenario, like hanging out with friends or meeting new people, where this strategy can help you feel more comfortable and confident.

Coping Strategy 3: _____

Situation: _____

Think about a time at home, like dealing with family disagreements or managing homework, where this strategy can make things easier for you.

REFLECT ON YOUR WINS

Think about a recent situation where you used one of your new coping strategies. How did it help you? **Write down how you felt before and after using the strategy.**

Before: _____

After: _____

PLAN A REWARD

Choose a fun way to reward yourself for your hard work. This could be anything from a favorite snack to a relaxing activity to spending time with friends. **Write down your reward plan here.**

Reward: _____

STAY MOTIVATED

Keep your coping strategies and progress in mind as you continue to face challenges. Remember, the more you practice, the better you'll get at handling stressful situations. **Write a positive note to yourself for future motivation to avoid avoidance!**

_____

_____

_____

_____

REFLECTIONS
REFLECTIONS

- **Exposure is one of the most effective ways to combat anxiety.** But it's also a tough thing to do. It involves moving into fear instead of moving away from it. Avoidance is easy and comfortable, but exposure is how you create change and get control of your worries.

- **Some days will be easier than others.** That is a normal part of the process. Keep pushing yourself, make sure you use all of your tools and skills, and know that it takes time. Overcoming fears isn't a race, and each person has their own pace. The key is to do it in a planned and strategic way instead of going to the biggest fear and trying to tackle it all at once. That doesn't work. As you practice, you will get better and better at facing your anxiety. Know that as hard as exposure is, it pays off tenfold. You've got this.

CHAPTER 9

KINDNESS UNLOCKED

Your Guide to Self-Compassion

matthew is a sixteen-year-old who is having a hard time. His mood has been lower recently, and his negative thoughts seem to be growing and growing. He has a constant internal dialogue where he berates himself for not measuring up to his own impossible expectations, finds fault with everything he does, and constantly criticizes himself for not doing or being enough. matthew would never speak to another person in the way he speaks to himself, but that doesn't stop him from constantly criticizing and demeaning himself. He has this belief that if he isn't criticizing himself, he isn't being honest with himself; if he isn't pushing himself and finding fault, then he might not realize all of his mistakes and issues. It's almost like he views his constant self-criticism as protecting him from forgetting about or not noticing his mistakes.

One night matthew's sister notices him staring into space. She asks him what's wrong, and he tells her that he did badly on his recent math test and feels like he is failing at everything. She suggests a technique from her mindfulness group: self-compassion. matthew isn't sure whether self-compassion is realistic for him or even a good idea. How could being kind to himself make him achieve more? It seems more likely that it will make him stop caring and do even worse. But at this point he is feeling so low, he's willing to try anything—even his sister's idea about self-compassion.

As matthew starts learning about self-compassion, he realizes it's really about treating himself as he would treat a friend—with kindness and understanding rather than blame and criticism. The first step is to pay attention to the critical voice in his head and to catch it when it's telling him he's not good enough, smart enough, or just not enough. Instead of letting the negative voice control how he feels, thinks, and acts, he starts to change the dialogue. He doesn't start randomly praising himself for no reason, but he does start to speak to himself as he would talk to a friend. And that makes a difference in how he feels.

Next, he starts to write down three specific things he did well each day. These can be related to anything: school, sports, friends, or family. Over time, Matthew notices a shift. He doesn't feel so stressed and overwhelmed. He finds himself catching the moments where he feels good and successful. He still works hard and aims high, but he doesn't beat himself up when things don't go perfectly. He understands that being kind to himself doesn't mean making excuses or ignoring his mistakes; rather, it's about giving himself the chance to grow, learn, and get better. Self-compassion turned out to be the best and kindest way to change.

Self-compassion is a deliberate technique where you practice treating yourself with kindness, concern, and forgiveness. When things go wrong, or when you notice something about yourself you don't like, self-compassion means you notice it and respond with kindness to yourself. It may or may not surprise you to know that most of us are not great at self-compassion. We tend to be far more critical of ourselves than we are of other people, and it turns out that self-criticism actually has a negative impact on how we perform at school, home, and with friends.

HOW IT WORKS

Kristin Neff, PhD, is a well-known researcher who has focused her career on understanding self-compassion. Her book *Self-Compassion: The Proven Power of Being Kind to Yourself* describes how self-compassion involves three key elements:

1. **SELF-KINDNESS VS. SELF-JUDGMENT:** This means you are gentle with yourself, rather than critical, when confronted with personal failings.

2. **COMMON HUMANITY VS. ISOLATION:** When you understand that suffering, feeling inadequate, and failure are universal and part of the shared human experience, you feel less isolated with your pain.

3. **MINDFULNESS VS. OVERIDENTIFICATION:** Mindfulness (as you already know) is a nonjudgmental and open state of mind in which you observe your thoughts and feelings as they are, without trying to suppress or deny them.

Dr. Neff suggest that self-compassion can make life feel better. It can reduce anxiety and depression, lower stress, and help us take care of ourselves (sleep, exercise, and eating well). When people are compassionate with themselves, they're less likely to be afraid of failure. Many of us think the opposite—that if we aren't hard on ourselves, we won't get anything done. Instead, the practice of self-compassion can lead to greater personal growth and achievement.

Self-compassion is definitely not about making everything rainbows and ponies. It's not about ignoring mistakes or accepting less from yourself than you're capable of. It's about acknowledging that everyone has challenges and that it's okay not to be perfect. Self-compassion is a practice; the more you work on being compassionate toward yourself, the more natural it becomes. And as with any skill, it gets stronger the more you use it. The goal is to find a balance where you can be motivated to grow without unnecessary self-criticism that can hold you back.

STRATEGY: FEED THE RIGHT WOLF

There is an old and wise proverb attributed to Native American communities about two wolves. In the proverb, the elder tells a child that we all have two wolves inside of us. These wolves are in constant battle with each other. One wolf represents anger, envy, greed, meanness, arrogance, and ego. The other wolf represents love, kindness, compassion, generosity, and truth. The child asks the elder which one of the wolves wins the battle. The elder responds: "The one you feed."

EXERCISE · WHICH WOLF DO YOU FEED?

Look at your own internal wolves and explore which one you feed. **In the chart below, write down the "food" you give each wolf—thoughts and behaviors that make each one stronger.**

WOLF #1: CRITICISM	WOLF #2: COMPASSION

Reflect on what each wolf says to you when faced with a challenge or mistake. **Write down their messages.**

Messages from Criticism Wolf: _____

_____

_____

Messages from Compassion Wolf: _____

_____

_____

Decide which wolf's message is more helpful for your growth and well-being. **Circle the wolf you choose to feed moving forward. If you want, draw this wolf in the space below and make them extra fancy and beautiful.** This could be a tiara, a cape, or anything you can imagine to highlight this wolf's awesomeness.

EXERCISE | STRENGTHEN THE COMPASSION WOLF

For one week, actively feed the Compassion Wolf. **At the end of each day, write down three or four compassionate statements that you said to yourself or wish you had said to yourself.** These might include:

"It's okay not to be perfect in everything."

"I'm going to talk to myself like I would to a good friend who's struggling."

"Everyone messes up sometimes, me included."

"I will be patient with myself; I am doing the best I can right now."

"I'm learning from my challenges and that's actually how I move forward."

"My feelings matter and I give myself permission to feel them and express them."

SUNDAY: _____

_____

_____

MONDAY: _____

_____

_____

TUESDAY: _____

_____

_____

WEDNESDAY: _____

_____

THURSDAY: _____

_____

FRIDAY: _____

_____

SATURDAY: _____

_____

After a week of working hard to feed the Compassion Wolf, what has changed?

_____

_____

_____

Create a visual reminder, like a small card with an image of the choice of which wolf to feed, to carry with you or place in a visible spot like next to your bed. This will help you understand how what you say to yourself gives power to either the positive or the negative. When you recognize that you have two "wolves" within you and consciously choose which one to feed, you get to be in charge. You have control. The way you choose to speak to yourself influences which aspects of your character you strengthen and cultivate.

STRATEGY: LETTER TO LOVELY YOU

This strategy asks you to craft a letter to yourself to foster kindness, compassion, and understanding. This letter will be rooted in Dr. Neff's research that highlights the importance of self-kindness, common humanity, and mindfulness. It may sound complicated initially, but give it a try. I think it will make more sense and feel more meaningful as you get into it.

EXERCISE LETTER TO LOVELY YOU

Take a few deep breaths to center yourself. Think of a recent situation that triggered self-criticism. **Jot a few notes below to remind yourself of the situation, your emotions, and your thoughts at the time. These are just notes, nothing formal.**

_____

_____

_____

Now that you have a rough idea of the situation you are going to address, start writing your letter. Use the following space as your stationary (feel free to decorate it). Use the following format as a guide.

GREETING

Start with a compassionate greeting to yourself. This means acknowledging your current feelings without judgment.

> "Dear [Your Name], I see that you're feeling anxious about the upcoming exams, and that's completely understandable. It's okay to feel this way."

> "[Your Name], I notice you're dealing with some tough emotions right now, and I want to tell you that it's okay to feel unsettled. You're going through a lot."

"Hey [Your Name], it looks like you're being really hard on yourself after what happened. It's natural to feel upset, and it's okay to be kind to yourself in this moment."

"[Your Name], I see you're feeling disappointed because things didn't go as planned. It's perfectly fine to have these feelings, and it's important to remember that they don't define you."

FIRST PARAGRAPH: KINDNESS

In the first paragraph, extend kindness to yourself. Address the self-critical thoughts and reframe them with kindness like you would for a friend. This might look like:

"I understand that you're feeling like you didn't do enough on your project, but you actually did work hard and put real effort into the project. I see your hard work, and it's enough. It's great to aim for success, but don't forget to recognize the progress you've already made."

SECOND PARAGRAPH: COMMON HUMANITY

In the second paragraph, write about how your experiences connect you to others. Remind yourself that you are not alone in your struggles. This could look like:

"Sometimes it feels like I'm the only one struggling with these feelings of not being enough, but when I look around, I realize that's not true. Everyone has moments where they doubt themselves and everyone faces challenges. I'm not alone. Every person has felt overwhelmed or uncertain at some point. Every single person. When I remember this, it helps me feel connected to others and less alone."

THIRD PARAGRAPH: MINDFULNESS

In the third paragraph, write mindfully about your feelings, acknowledging them without trying to change or judge them. This might be similar to:

"In this moment, I am taking a deep breath and pausing to notice how I feel. I am aware of a tightness in my chest, and it feels familiar. It feels like anxiety. I recognize this feeling and allow it to be there, without pushing it away or telling myself that I shouldn't feel this way. This feeling is temporary. I can acknowledge the discomfort of this feeling and know that it is okay to feel anxious. I observe my anxiety, and know it is okay."

COMPASSIONATE CLOSURE

Conclude the letter with words of support and encouragement for the future. Sign the letter with kindness and compassion.

"This feeling is uncomfortable, but I've done hard things before and I can get through this too. I have lots of strengths and good qualities and I am learning how to deal with frustrations and disappointments, just like everyone else in the world."

Writing a self-compassion letter allows you to honestly and compassionately express yourself and examine your experience. It lets you acknowledge that we all make mistakes and that we all share a common human experience. It encourages mindfulness and fosters a gentler and more supportive relationship with yourself. This written exercise can be something you return to when you need a reminder of the importance of self-compassion. It can feel silly or embarrassing initially, but this is a great tool for self-reflection and self-compassion.

STRATEGY: BUILD AN ACCEPTANCE GARDEN

For this strategy, you are going to build and grow a compassionate mindset through the metaphor of gardening. This idea comes from the ACT literature and is based on the practice of allowing your thoughts and feelings as they are rather than fighting them or feeling guilty about them. Ideally, you can accept your experiences without self-criticism and with compassion.

Building, growing, and maintaining an "acceptance garden" is a way to visually understand and practice self-compassion. When you are practicing acceptance, you are encouraging yourself to accept your thoughts and feelings, understanding that they are not who you are. Acceptance allows you to gain perspective and step back, catch the instinctive criticisms and judgments, and change to language and emotion that supports growth. Self-growth is a continuous process that takes ongoing effort, but it is well worth it.

 **EXERCISE** BUILD AN ACCEPTANCE GARDEN

PREPARE THE SOIL

Write a list of negative thoughts, self-judgments, or criticisms you say to yourself.

Example: "I always say the wrong thing."

PLANT SEEDS OF ACCEPTANCE

For each judgment, plant a "seed" of acceptance by writing a statement that acknowledges the thought or feeling without trying to change it.

Example: *"It's rare I say things just right, but I mostly do okay."*

_____

_____

_____

_____

TEND WITH KINDNESS

Write down what you can do today to show kindness to yourself, nurturing the seeds of acceptance.

Example: *"I am going to write down three specific things that I did really well today."*

_____

_____

_____

_____

GROW THE GARDEN

For each seed of acceptance, draw a sprout that represents your commitment to being kind to yourself when you experience that thought or feeling.

DAILY MAINTENANCE

Each day, take a moment to observe your garden. Notice whether (and when) any old judgments return and how your seeds of acceptance are growing. **Add any new seeds as needed.**

SUNDAY: _____

MONDAY: _____

TUESDAY: _____

WEDNESDAY: _____

THURSDAY: _____

FRIDAY: _____

SATURDAY: _____

REFLECT ON GROWTH

At the end of the week, reflect on the growth of your acceptance garden. How has cultivating acceptance and kindness affected how you treat yourself?

_____

_____

_____

_____

_____

REFLECTIONS

REFLECTIONS

- **Self-compassion is a powerful tool.** Self-compassion can change how we view ourselves, how we view challenges, and how we view our place in the world. Criticizing and judging ourselves is a habit many of us have without realizing it. When we actively practice self-compassion, we treat ourselves better. The better we treat ourselves, the better we feel and the better we perform. We can see our mistakes not as failures, but as something everyone experiences. Rather than getting stuck in a cycle of shame, we can use self-compassion to move forward.

- **Self-compassion involves three parts:** being gentle with ourselves instead of critical, remembering that all people have challenges, and seeing our thoughts and feelings clearly without judging them. Self-compassion can help us feel less anxious or depressed, lower our stress, and encourage us to take better care of ourselves. We'll be less afraid of failing and will experience greater personal growth. Self-compassion is a skill and a practice, and the time to start is right now.

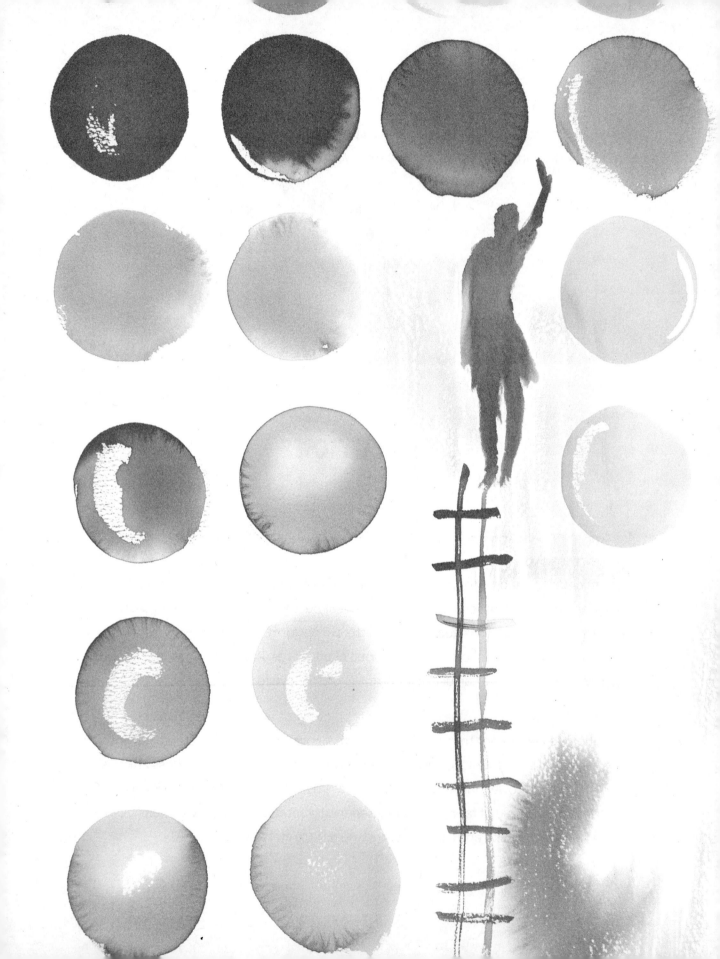

CHAPTER 10

CHALLENGE CHAMPION

Turning Obstacles into Opportunities

Lena is a fifteen-year-old high-school student who is extremely stressed about schoolwork. She is in her junior year, and it feels like she can't keep up with a never-ending number of assignments, tests, and projects. In the next week she has a huge history project due, two quizzes, and one major test. Her stress levels are rising, and she knows she needs a way to figure this out. She decides that learning more about problem-solving techniques is the best place to start.

Problem solving is pretty self-explanatory: it's a set of skills focused on solving problems, but the skills themselves are the key part. In real problem solving, you are learning skills to find solutions to problems that actually work. You aren't just going to get through this one period of time; rather, you learn a mindset that you can apply to any challenging time. Problem solving involves learning a clear and structured way to identify problems, break them down, form a plan, and make the stress much less overwhelming.

Problem solving is a major component of CBT. You learn the basic strategies for identifying problems (which is harder than it sounds) and then work to come up with multiple ways to solve them. Problem solving is a way to take something big and overwhelming that is hanging over your head in a whirlwind of stress and break it down into clear and identifiable steps. Rather than walking around thinking, "I'm so stressed, I'm so stressed," you come up with practical steps you can take to reduce the stress and solve the problem.

The best thing about problem solving for Lena is that it gives her a feeling of control when everything feels overwhelming. Problem solving helps you take charge of the situation and move forward in a useful way. It's not about fixing everything at once—it's about changing how you look at the situation so you feel more in control. The more you practice, the better you get, and the next time something stressful comes up, you'll be more prepared.

Problem solving is a seriously useful skill that helps you navigate challenges and find effective solutions. It's not just about solving a math problem or completing a homework assignment; it's about developing a mindset that enables you to tackle any obstacle that comes your way. When you approach problems with a clear and structured method, you can break them down into manageable parts and reduce the overwhelming feeling that often comes with stress.

Problem solving sounds basic and mundane, and that causes people to underestimate the power of the skill. Problem solving is often seen as just another task rather than a necessary life skill. Knowing how to solve problems consistently and effectively is a powerful skill that can significantly (in a good way) improve your life.

Problem solving is a key component of CBT. By identifying and addressing problems proactively, you can prevent the buildup of stress and anxiety. This approach teaches you to think critically and develop practical solutions, which changes your thoughts, feelings, and actions.

HOW IT WORKS

When you're facing a problem, the first step is to figure out what is really going on. This means looking at the problem from all angles; if this was an easy problem to solve, you wouldn't be struggling. Acknowledge that it's complicated, and start to break it down.

IDENTIFY THE PROBLEM: Effective problem solving begins with identifying and clearly defining the problem. This helps you understand what you're dealing with.

BRAINSTORM SOLUTIONS: This involves thinking of all the different ways you could tackle the issue, without judging any ideas too quickly. The goal is to generate a wide range of options, and some of these may be a little bit out there. That's okay.

EVALUATE YOUR IDEAS: After brainstorming, the next step is to evaluate each potential solution. This means looking at the pros and cons of each option and considering factors such as time, resources, and possible outcomes. It's important to choose a solution that is realistic and achievable given your specific circumstances.

TAKE ACTION: Once you've chosen the best solution, it's time to take action. Create a detailed plan that outlines the steps you need to take. Setting small, manageable goals can help keep you on track and make the task feel less daunting. It's also helpful to set deadlines for each step to ensure that you stay motivated and focused.

REVIEW THE RESULTS: After implementing the solution, it's important to review the results. Reflect on what worked well and what didn't. If the problem persists or new challenges arise, you can revisit your list of potential solutions and try a different approach. This continuous process of evaluation and adjustment helps you improve your problem-solving skills over time.

STRATEGY: PROBLEM SOLVING 101

Here's an example of how problem solving might look for Lena:

1. **IDENTIFY THE PROBLEM:** Lena first needs to pinpoint the primary source of her stress. It turns out to be an upcoming project that significantly affects her class grade. Recognizing that she feels most overwhelmed in the evenings when she plans to work on her project is a crucial insight.

2. **BRAINSTORM SOLUTIONS:** Lena next explores various strategies to manage her project. She can break the project into manageable parts, ask her teacher for guidance, or allocate time each morning when she feels more energized and less stressed. She should write down all potential solutions and consider each one without dismissing them right away.

3. **EVALUATE YOUR IDEAS:** After creating a list of possible solutions, Lena thinks about the pros and cons of each one. Then she picks one to try first: working on a section of the project every morning. By committing to this step, she can make the

task feel less daunting and hopefully reduce her stress. A helpful step is to write down the commitment on a visual reminder that you see daily.

4. **TAKE ACTION:** Lena gets up half an hour earlier each day for a week and works on her project.

5. **REVIEW THE RESULTS:** After a few days of getting up early, Lena realizes that she is too tired when she gets to school, so she decides to try another idea on her list: asking her teacher for help.

After Lena tries her second idea, talking to the teacher, she would review the results and see whether that was helpful. If not, she would return to her list of ideas and try again.

EXERCISE IDENTIFY THE PROBLEM

What problem can you identify that is complicated, hard to solve, and interfering with life in some way?

_____

What stands out about this problem?

_____

Does this problem stay consistent, or does it change in different situations? What helps and what hurts it?

_____

How do you feel when you think about this problem?

_____

What are your negative automatic thoughts (NATs) when considering this problem?

What would it look like if this problem were solved? Describe.

Once you've got a clear picture of the problem, it's time to come up with ideas for how to handle it. This is the brainstorming stage, and it's truly a time for no bad ideas.

EXERCISE BRAINSTORM SOLUTIONS

Write down all the possible ways you could respond to the problem, even if they seem ridiculous or unlikely; let your brain open up and explore. The goal is to think of as many solutions as possible without judging them. This gives you options to choose from and helps you see solutions that you might not have thought of before.

EXERCISE EVALUATE YOUR IDEAS

After you've come up with a number of ideas, look at each one and think about how it could work. In this stage, you take the role of a critical thinker and examine each idea individually. By carefully evaluating your ideas, you can make more effective decisions and move closer to your goals.

IDEA	STRENGTHS	WEAKNESSES	SHORT-TERM IMPACT	LONG-TERM IMPACT	IS THIS IDEA WORK-ABLE? Y/N
Get up early before school to work on my project.	I can carve out time to devote to my project when I don't have other homework to worry about.	Losing sleep time in the morning might make me tired.	I get a lot done on the first few days.	I am tired the rest of the day and it ac-cumulates during the week.	No

TAKE ACTION

This phase is important—it's about making thoughtful choices, not just going with the first option that comes to mind. Consider what could go right with each idea, but also what challenges might arise. Choose one or two ideas that seem the best, and plan how you can try them out.

Chosen Idea 1:

Plan:

Chosen Idea 2:

Plan:

Now it's time for action. This is when you actually try out one of the chosen solutions.

REVIEW THE RESULTS

Which solution did you try?

_____

What steps did you take to implement the solution?

_____

_____

_____

What was the outcome? Did it work?

_____

_____

_____

How do you feel now compared to before trying problem solving?

_____

If it didn't work as well as you hoped, why not?

_____

_____

_____

What will you do differently next time?

_____

_____

Remember, problem solving is often about trying different things and learning from what didn't work. Each time you try a solution, you learn something new, and that brings you one step closer to finding the key that really works for you. Solving problems is a process, and it's okay to try, learn, and try again.

STRATEGY: EXTERNALIZE THE PROBLEM

One of the key ideas in CBT is to externalize the problem—make it something outside of you. This way, you can deal with it more effectively. When you externalize a problem, you create distance between yourself and the issue, which can make it feel less overwhelming. It allows you to view the problem objectively, as something separate from your identity. This perspective can reduce its emotional impact and help you think more clearly about how to address it. By seeing the problem as a character or creature, you can better understand its influence on your thoughts and actions and develop strategies to manage it more effectively. This technique helps you shift from feeling controlled by the problem to feeling empowered to tackle it.

 **EXERCISE** EXTERNALIZE THE PROBLEM

NAME THE PROBLEM

What is the main problem you're facing?

_____

_____

_____

_____

IMAGINE THE PROBLEM AS A CHARACTER

Think of your problem as a character or creature. **Then, flesh out that character by choosing a name and describing what it sounds like, where it lives, what its job is, how its friends would portray it, and anything else you want to say about it.**

_____

_____

_____

_____

Draw your character or creature.

INTERVIEW YOUR PROBLEM

Ask your character some questions to understand it better.

Why do you exist?

_____

_____

What do you want from me?

_____

_____

How do you affect my actions or feelings?

_____

_____

What can I do to get you to change or transform?

_____

_____

PLAN YOUR STRATEGY

Think about the challenges you might face dealing with this problem and how you can overcome them. **Write down a challenge and your strategy for handling it.**

CHALLENGE	STRATEGY

By externalizing the problem, you step back and see your problem through a different perspective. Hopefully it helped you gain insight and new ideas for managing it. Remember, it's okay to have fun with this—sometimes a different perspective is all you need to find a solution.

REFLECTIONS
REFLECTIONS

- **Learning to solve problems effectively can really make a big difference.** It's a little annoying at first, but once you get used to the steps, you have a clear tool for working through tough situations.

- **Using problem-solving skills helps you manage stress and prevents issues from piling up.** When you tackle problems head-on, you not only find solutions but also build confidence and resilience. This proactive approach keeps you in control and stops minor issues from becoming major ones.

- **Problem solving is a continuous process, not a one-time fix.** It involves trying different strategies, learning from each experience, and getting better over time. Not every solution will be perfect, but that's okay—each attempt is a step toward improvement.

Elisa Nebolsine, LCSW, practices cognitive behavioral therapy (CBT) and eye movement desensitization and reprocessing (EMDR) in her Alexandria, VA, private practice. She is adjunct faculty at the Beck Institute for Cognitive Behavior Therapy, and an award-winning clinician in the Washington, DC, area. Elisa is author of *The Grit Workbook for Kids* and *Your Amazing Teen Brain*.

Foreword writer *Matthew McKay, PhD*, is a professor at the Wright Institute in Berkeley, CA. He has authored and coauthored numerous books, including *Thoughts and Feelings*, *The Dialectical Behavior Therapy Skills Workbook*, and *Self-Esteem*. He specializes in the cognitive behavioral treatment of anxiety and depression.

Did you know there are **free tools** you can download for this book?

Free tools are things like **worksheets**, **guided meditation exercises**, and **more** that will help you get the most out of your book.

You can download free tools for this book—whether you bought or borrowed it, in any format, from any source—from the New Harbinger website. All you need is a NewHarbinger.com account. Just use the URL provided in this book to view the free tools that are available for it. Then, click on the "download" button for the free tool you want, and follow the prompts that appear to log in to your NewHarbinger.com account and download the material.

You can also save the free tools for this book to your **Free Tools Library** so you can access them again anytime, just by logging in to your account! Just look for this button on the book's free tools page.

+ Save this to my free tools library

If you need help accessing or downloading free tools, visit **newharbinger.com/faq** or contact us at **customerservice@newharbinger.com**.